'Full of great s   lethal
business of illegal alcohol – Henry Jeffreys, *The Guardian Best Drink Books of 2015*

'Evok[es], with its tales of gin being piped in alleyways, a mood o   ostalgic Blitz-era gentility' – Stephen Bayley, *Spectator*

'   engaging, witty and informative read for anyone
i   rested in the colourful and exciting history of booze'
    infestival.com

    {any laugh out loud moments . . . I absolutely loved the
    cipes. . . . It's such an interesting book that I am sure I
    ill pick it up again for many years to come. It has certainly
    ade drinking whisky and gin much more interesting . . .
    ist the right amount of history and humour'
    The Book Magnet

    for boozy, literary-minded dreamers . . . a lively and
    ngaging read' – Countrywives.co.uk

    'm forever fascinated by the underground, and the
    ub-cultural drinking habits of bad old Blighty are a
    p-roaring read' – King Adz, author of *The Urban Cookbook*
    nd *Street Knowledge*

    loved everything about this book; the enthusiasm it
    brings to its subject, the try this at home approach, its
    humour, and the stories it brings to life. It really has a lot
    to recommend it' – desperatereader.blogspot.uk

'A damn fun read . . . I love the mix of historical facts with recipes and personal stories from the characters involved. And the characters we meet on the way are fascinating – as are the ingenious lengths they go to in order to conceal their illicit booze making from the authorities'
– Madame J-Mo

'Alchemist and drinks genius Ruth Ball has written a thrilling history of people and events surrounding the intoxicating world of spirits' – Lemonaste blog

REBELLIOUS SPIRITS

AUDACIOUS TALES OF DRINKING ON THE WRONG SIDE OF THE LAW

RUTH BALL

First published 2015 by
Elliott and Thompson Limited
27 John Street
London WC1N 2BX
www.eandtbooks.com

This paperback edition first published in 2018

ISBN: 978-178396-379-9

9 8 7 6 5 4 3 2 1

A catalogue record for this book is available from the British Library.

Typesetting: Marie Doherty
Cover design: © www.patrickknowlesdesign.com
Printed and bound by CPI Group (UK) Ltd, Croydon, CR0 4YY

CONTENTS

INTRODUCTION

Britain is a nation of enthusiastic drinkers. You don't have to look far to see that. In 2016 around 30 million Brits had a drink and, of those, almost 5 million drank on at least five days of the week. Small villages start national campaigns to save their only pub, the heart of the community, and in larger towns driving directions are often given using the pubs as landmarks. A friend's house will be 'left at The Rising Sun, straight on past The Crown but if you reach The Haymakers you've gone too far'.

We love our booze, and woe betide anyone who tries to interfere with it. Any attempt to regulate, ban or limit supply has only resulted in rebellious behaviour. We have a long and proud history, filled with wonderfully colourful stories, of people determined to fly in the face of authority, and continue making, selling, buying and, of course, consuming our favourite spirits, whether it's someone selling gin through pipes and over windowsills in a London back alley; hiding stashes in a secret chamber in the walls of a peat burner's hut on an Irish bog; a lone figure standing guard on a Cornish clifftop waiting for a smuggler's signal; or dodging bombs and shrapnel running whisky in the Blitz.

The history of spirits in Britain has more illicit in it than licit. The most famous whisky brands have huge, mysterious holes in their official histories, times when writing down what they were doing would have been too dangerous, so that much is a mystery even to their owners. The British government even tried to outlaw drinking gin at the cost of thousands of pounds and the loss of what little popularity it had. The strictest control measures have always failed. The rebellious spirit of spirit drinkers refuses to be quelled.

Beer and wine are all very well for a work night out or your cousin's wedding, but it has always been spirits that accompany naughtiness and rule-breaking. No gunslinger ever burst into a saloon and demanded half a pint of craft lager; no gangster ever set up an illegal wine press in their bathtub. Spirits are the true drink of the underworld. Such a powerful drink in such a small package: the feel of that first sip like liquid fire warming right down to your toes, the knowledge that a pint of it would mean certain oblivion. We know that it's wrong, but that is what is so tantalisingly right.

In writing this history I have delved into archives, scoured newspapers and listened carefully to the rich oral history passed from bartender to bartender in order to find some of the best stories and amazing characters behind the black-market trade in spirits. Sometimes the sources were a little questionable – the words of thieves and smugglers – but these are the stories as they were recorded by the people who lived them, complete with their own embellishments and wild claims. To give you a taste of the history and bring it alive, the stories are accompanied by authentic recipes for drinks of the era – along with adaptations by me, the Alchemist, to make them safe and legal. Follow them carefully for a genuine taste of history.

Finally, before you immerse yourself in this very British history of spirits and discover a new world, pour yourself one of those classic American Prohibition-era cocktails. I recommend the Sidecar, a popular cocktail in the more glamorous New York speakeasies of the 1920s. Supplied by gangsters and sipped by the rich and the famous, it was strong, simple and heavily flavoured with citrus to disguise the poor quality of bootleg bathtub brandy. Drink furtively while fully prepared to flee at the first sign of a raid by the fuzz.

SIDECAR

*2 parts brandy (a cheap brandy for authenticity
or a VSOP cognac for pleasure)
1 part orange brandy (or Cointreau)
1 part lemon juice*

*Shake over ice and strain into a chilled Martini glass. Now sit
yourself in a leather wing chair, light up a good cigar and sip
slowly as you read this book.*

CHAPTER ONE

MONKS AND
MONASTERIES

For a long time there were no illicit spirits in Britain. Spirits cannot break the law when there are no laws to break, and laws about spirits cannot exist until spirits exist themselves. So before the story of illicit spirits in Britain can be told, I have to tell the story of how spirits came to be, and of the journey they took to reach one small windswept isle on the edge of Europe – an isle inhabited by people who were badly in need of a dram or two to keep out the cold.

The true origins of spirits have often been debated. Some claim they were being distilled in Egypt as the pyramids were built, others that arrack has been produced in Sri Lanka for three millennia. There's little proof for any of these theories; most are based on a line or two in a single book that could be interpreted this way or that. The discovery could even have been made more than once, miles

1

and centuries apart. The version I've chosen to tell is my favourite and just as likely to be true as any other.

Like many great inventions, it all began in Greece over 2,000 years ago. Unfortunately, once discovered, the invention was forgotten again for more than half of those years. Or rather, not exactly forgotten, but kept a closely guarded secret by a mystic sect who based their entire religion on getting very drunk. You could call that behaviour selfish or you could just call it normal behaviour for the constantly intoxicated. Whatever the reasons, this religious secret-keeping meant that it wasn't until the thirteenth century that anyone else in the world really got to have a proper drink. To make matters worse, those in the sect who knew the secret didn't even use the spirit for drinking.

The first spirits in the world, instead of being consumed in the usual manner, were used for a very special ceremony. An initiate would be brought before a gathering of the sect and neat spirit would be poured over their head and shoulders. Then, to test whether they were truly under the god's protection, they would be set alight.

With luck, the initiate would be kept safe from serious burns by a special property that most, but not quite all, spirits have. Spirits are high in alcohol compared to fermented drinks like wine – they have enough alcohol to catch alight and to burn for a while, but they are still usually mostly water. When something is soaked in spirit and set alight then the alcohol will burn off, leaving behind enough water to stop even something flammable, such as paper or human hair, from catching on fire. However, if the spirit is too strong (around 60 per cent abv or above) then there is not enough water left for protection, and the soaked thing – or person – will scorch and burn. With no reliable way for the cult to test the strength of the spirits they were producing, this had the potential to be a dangerous initiation.

The whole ritual just goes to show what kinds of risky ideas result from the overconsumption of wine. Most Ancient Greeks drank theirs watered and believed that anyone who drank undiluted wine would go mad. So it's probably best not to take the risk and to stick to a nice, safe dry Martini.

The deity who inspired this befuddled and dangerous devotion was Dionysus, god of wine, the vine and all moist fruits. His sects were found throughout Greece and were many and varied in nature. As you might imagine, the worship of the god of drink and mayhem was not an organised affair but performed here and there, this way and that way, by any who felt his calling. But there is one sect in particular that is recorded as having performed the spirit-burning ceremony and they came from Delphi.

Delphi was a shrine that was devoted primarily to the sun god Apollo, but it was also teeming with other religions, cults and sects crammed many to a street. There was nothing particularly unusual about the worshippers all setting up side by side. In a society that accepted the existence of many gods, the average citizen would visit all of them, trying to stay on their good side. By modern standards, the Delphi cult of Dionysus was unusually secretive, obsessive and, well, completely barking mad; in Ancient Delphi it was just one among many.

People like to think that the Ancient Greeks were all like Socrates, great philosophers; but for every sensible and serious great thinker or inventor in Ancient Greece, there were at least ten people dedicating their lives to the worship of a deity who could only be appeased by a precise calendar of complex ritual. The two weren't even separate – it is just that we tend to remember the works that we think of as important, and forget about the rest.

Everyone knows Pythagoras for his theorem, a brilliant mathematical equation for working out the hypotenuse of a right-angled triangle. Not many know that he was also the founder of a religious cult. This cult believed in reincarnation, vegetarianism, truthfulness and that the soul was fed by music. All very reasonable beliefs and surely a credit to any religion – except that they also believed that you should only have sex in the winter and that you should never eat beans because they are made of the same material as human beings. Legend even has it that Pythagoras died as he was fleeing from his burning house, chased by his enemies: because he refused to risk damaging the beans by running through a bean field to escape, he was killed. Even the mathematical discoveries for which we now remember him were the result of exploring the mystic properties of triangles. Pythagoras believed that the important spiritual properties of triangles could be better understood only by developing their mathematics. Practical uses were a happy side effect.

So while the beliefs of the Dionysians who first discovered spirits were strange by our standards, they were fairly usual by those of the time. Discovering how to extract the alcohol from wine and using it for worship was a logical product of their beliefs – it brought them closer to their god by concentrating his greatest gift. The fact that spirits were also a delicious drink was just another happy practical side effect. Setting fire to themselves rather than drinking it was less obviously logical but it must have made some kind of sense to them.

While most of the local population who wished to worship would only come to the major ceremonies of the cult of Dionysus once or twice a year, the followers who devoted themselves completely to the god and lived permanently in the sect were the only ones who would have taken part in the ceremony of the spirit. The initiates named themselves the Maenads, after the most important members of the god's retinue. The mystical Maenads took the form of beautiful women, but if angered by the failure of the temple to present the correct offerings, they could grow talons and go on a rampage. All the passions of mortals would be whipped up into a frenzy of sex, intoxication, madness and bloodlust. To prevent that terrible possibility, the mortal Maenads stuck carefully to their two-yearly cycle of offerings and rituals.

Since Delphi was primarily dedicated to the sun god Apollo, it was especially appropriate for the Dionysians to have a presence there. The myth told that for four months every winter Apollo would ride off in his fiery chariot to visit a mystical race in the north, leaving his brother Dionysus in charge. In the first year that Apollo left, Dionysus was awoken by his handmaidens as Dionysus Liknites – Dionysus of birth. He breathed life into the grape vines so that they would begin to sprout and show new growth just as his short reign was coming to a close. It ended with his violent death just before the return of Apollo, when a love affair gone very wrong resulted in him being torn limb from limb by Titans. His followers reputedly celebrated this by tearing a live goat apart with their bare hands. Dionysus then descended into the underworld before being reborn the following year. The goat was not so lucky.

With the death of the god, the humans were left to gather the grapes and set them in vats to begin their fermentation. At the start of the next winter, just as fermentation was ending, Dionysus was reborn as Dionysus Chthonius – Dionysus of the underworld. This was when he breathed the sacred fire, alcohol, into the liquid, making it warming and intoxicating. The time had arrived for a great festival to celebrate the new wine that Dionysus had granted them. Wine was drunk year round, even though it would quickly deteriorate as the Greeks did not have particularly good preservation techniques. Since it could not be aged as modern wine usually is, it could be harsh and acidic. They drank it watered to prevent madness, and it was also often spiced and honeyed.

The practice of drinking sweetened, spiced wine was still common until well into the seventeenth century when improvements in winemaking techniques finally began to produce wines that were palatable without sweetening. This method is from a collection of Roman recipes, and although there are many earlier references to this type of wine, it is the earliest complete written recipe.

SPICED WINE: THE ORIGINAL
(TRANSLATED FROM LATIN)

The composition of excellent spiced wine. Into a copper bowl put 6 sextarii of honey and 2 sextarii of wine; heat on a slow fire, constantly stirring the mixture with a whip. At the boiling point add a dash of cold wine, retire from stove and skim. Repeat this twice or three times, let it rest till the next day, and skim again. Then add 4 oz of crushed pepper, 3 scruples of mastich, a drachm each of leaves and saffron, 5 drachms of roasted date stones crushed and previously soaking in wine to soften them. When this is properly done add 18 sextarii of light wine. To clarify it perfectly, add charcoal twice as often as necessary, which will draw together.

Apicius *(c. 4th century)*

THE ALCHEMIST'S VERSION

800g honey

3 litres cheap red wine

1 tbsp ground allspice

¼ tsp ground star anise

½ tsp saffron

1 bay leaf

1 tbsp crushed toasted almonds

For authenticity, use the cheapest red wine you can find. I do mean really cheap red wine. The kind you see in corner shops, three for a tenner. That kind of cheap.

In a large pan, mix all of the honey with 200ml of the wine and bring to the boil. Once it comes to the boil, turn down to a very low simmer and add all the remaining ingredients, except for the additional wine. Cover and continue to simmer gently for an hour; or you can simply take it off the heat immediately and leave it to sit for a day at room temperature.

Once cool, this produces a concentrated spiced wine that can be bottled and kept in the fridge for up to a year. Before drinking, mix the concentrated spiced wine with three times as much equally cheap red wine and an equal quantity of water (to prevent madness), then strain through a fine sieve or muslin.

The time when the wine was first ready to drink was a time of great celebration. Dionysus was returned and at his most powerful, bringing the gift of the wine that could be used to commune with him. His followers danced on Mount Parnassus, drank deeply and whipped themselves up into a drunken frenzy, taking on the aspect of the furious Maenads. Everyone could and would join in with this celebration of the new wine, a festival of drinking that has its echoes in the later and more famous Bacchanalia of Rome.

After the public festivities were done, the Maenads descended alone into Dionysus' tomb for the secret part of the ceremony. There they used a basic form of still to bring forth the pure spirit of the god (the alcohol) from the wine, and they poured it on the heads of the new initiates for their trial by fire.

I really cannot recommend trying this ceremony for yourself. While the temperature is relatively safe for short periods, it is still hot, and if you fail to cover absolutely every inch of your head with spirit you'll find the dry patches of hair catching fire. The experience of getting vodka in your eyes is also really not to be recommended. However, if you do want to experience a little of the drama with less of the risk then you could give this Victorian parlour game a try. It is relatively safe but still to be played at your own risk and preferably played sober, or at least with sober supervision.

This description of the game is taken from Robert Chambers' *Book of Days*, an enormous collection of facts and trivia published in 1864, and I think it needs no translation:

> *One favourite Christmas sport, very generally played on Christmas Eve, has been handed down to us from time immemorial under the name of 'Snapdragon'. To our English readers this amusement is perfectly familiar, but it is almost unknown in Scotland, and it seems therefore desirable here to give a description of the pastime.*
>
> *A quantity of raisins are deposited in a large dish or bowl (the broader and shallower this is, the better), and brandy or some other spirit is poured over the fruit and ignited. The bystanders now endeavour, by turns, to grasp a raisin, by plunging their hands through the flames; and as this is somewhat of an arduous feat, requiring both courage and rapidity of action, a considerable amount of laughter and merriment is evoked at the expense of the unsuccessful competitors. . . .*
>
> *Whilst the sport of Snapdragon is going on, it is usual to extinguish all the lights in the room, so that the lurid glare from the flaming spirits may exercise to the full its weird-like effect.*

The cult of Dionysus was anarchic. They accepted and liberated women, slaves and outlaws. That kept them at the fringes of society, feared by those in authority. Still, they managed to continue practising even after Greece was conquered by Rome and throughout most of Roman rule. They were finally extinguished only when the Roman Empire converted to Christianity and began eliminating all of the old mystery religions. Followers of Dionysus fled into

Persia and Arabia with a great exodus of non-Christians of all kinds, taking their well-kept secret with them.

Distillation was one of the cult's most precious secrets and would never deliberately have been passed to outsiders. But the various mystery cults that were in exile together often merged, split and merged again with one another, and secrets did pass in this way to many different cults and religions. Somewhere along the way, the mystic secret of distillation arrived in the hands of a cult of Christian heretics called the Gnostics, who carried it though the Balkans into western Europe as one of their own religious secrets. Sadly, they were still not drinking the spirits they made – instead, just like the Greeks before them, they were using spirits to set fire to their heads.

The Gnostics as a sect were opposed to the wealth and power of the established Catholic Church, living and working instead with the poorest in the community. They also took one passage from the gospel of St John literally when they were performing baptisms: 'Except a man be born of water and of the spirit, he cannot enter into the kingdom of God.' So, using the secret of distillation learned from the Dionysians, the Gnostics would perform the normal baptism with holy water – but then they would perform a second baptism with fire by soaking themselves in distilled spirit and setting themselves alight.

Finally, the practice of distillation passed from the Gnostics to a similar Christian sect, the Cathars, who spread the practice throughout Germany, Italy and France.

The Cathars were much more widespread and less secretive than the previous tiny sects who had practised distillation. They did not restrict the secret to full-time members of the religious order but allowed it to be known to all of the faithful, including many who held other professions. Most importantly, there were many doctors who were Cathars and who, on learning of this 'holy spirit', began experimenting with it for medicinal use. When the Cathars were finally crushed by the Inquisition in the late thirteenth century, the secret had already been preserved in medical writings – along with a key to the religious secrets it supposedly held, written in code.

The instructions for distilling were set down in medical texts in plain language, accompanied by claims about the medicinal properties of spirits. They may not have been intended for use as real cures for real diseases but instead as a code for the mystical and religious properties of the spirit. The faithful were supposed to recognise this and be able to find the secret where it was safely hidden and preserved from the persecutions of the Catholic Church. The claims that spirits could 'ease an ancient pain in the head' were code for taking away the pain of original sin; that they could 'hold back old age and restore youth' meant the granting of eternal life for the spirit, and the ability to 'take away darkness, spots or cataract from the eyes' was the granting of the true sight of the faithful.

The secret of distillation lay hidden in these medical texts, which were kept in abbeys. The texts were faithfully copied and preserved by monks who dedicated themselves to the care of that written knowledge even though they often made no use of it themselves. Most orders were opposed to practising medicine, believing that only God should be able to heal, and so the medical books were of no use to them. Even if they had been practicing medicine, it would have been dangerous to be seen practising anything associated with the heretic Cathars while they were still remembered.

But by the beginning of the fourteenth century, that belief had begun to change. Many monasteries had changed their views of the practice of medicine, beginning to see it as part of their charitable work, and were trying to produce their own medicines to use. The Cathars had been largely forgotten. And there were the instructions for distilling spirits, just sitting forgotten and unused in most of the common medical texts. It surely could not be long before someone followed the recipe and spirits were finally made, known and drunk.

It was a Franciscan friar by the name of John of Rupescissa who, in the 1330s, finally rediscovered the lost art of distillation. What's more, as well as prescribing it for external use as the written recipes recommended, he advised that Christian princes should take barrels of it into battle and give it to their soldiers as it could 'make a man that is a coward hardy and strong if he drank but half a cupful'. After almost 2,000 years as nothing but a source of mystical fire, spirits were finally starting to be drunk for their intoxicating properties.

By the mid-fourteenth century medicinal spirits, under the name 'aqua vitae' (water of life), had spread throughout mainland Europe. As a medicine, aqua vitae came in three types: 'simple' – a raw, unflavoured spirit from a single distillation; 'composite' – flavoured with one or two herbs by redistillation or infusion; and 'perfect' – a complex recipe involving nine to thirteen redistillations over various herbs. The burning properties of simple spirits were also being rediscovered and they were used as a dramatic stage prop for the Christian 'mystery plays' popular in France, producing the flames for the burning bush that spoke to Moses.

Tracking down a copy of the aqua vitae perfectissima recipe was not an easy task, as most have been lost or are written in archaic German. Even after an English version was traced, the names of the spices had to be carefully decoded. Then the right methods and proportions to allow an approximation to be made without using a still had to be found. Altogether, this was the most difficult recipe to produce in this book, but it was also one of the most rewarding. Given the number and rarity of the spices involved, in the time it was written this recipe must have been so expensive that the cost itself reassured customers that it was a certain cure. In the Alchemist's version, some of the more obscure spices have been left in, but a more common spice that can sensibly be substituted is given in brackets. Rue and sermountain have been omitted as they are nearly impossible to find or to substitute for; but if you happen to have some in your garden, throw in a chopped tablespoon of those, too. Otherwise, with the wealth of flavours already included, you won't miss them.

AQUA VITAE PERFECTISSIMA: THE ORIGINAL

Fille thi viol ful of lyes of strong wiyn, & putte therto these poudris: poudir of canel, of clowes, of gyngyuer, of notemugges, of galyngale, of quibibis, of greyn de parys, of longe peper, of blake peper: alle these in powdir. Careawey, cirmunteyn, comyn, fenel, smallage, persile, sauge, myntis, ruwe, calamynte, origanum: and a half unce or moore or lasse, as thee likith. Pownd hem a litil, for it will be the betir, & put hem to these poudris, Thanne sette thi glas on the fier, sett on the houel, & kepe it wel that the hete come not o it; & sette thervndir a viol, & kepe the watir.

Curye on Inglysch (c. 14th century)

THE ALCHEMIST'S VERSION

350ml brandy

½ tsp ground cinnamon

5 whole cloves

½ tsp ground ginger

½ tsp freshly grated nutmeg

3 slices fresh galangal (or additional ½ tsp ground ginger)

½ tsp cubeb pepper (or allspice)

1 tsp whole grains of paradise (or ¼ tsp whole green cardamom seeds)

¼ tsp ground long pepper (or ¼ tsp ground black pepper)

¼ tsp ground black pepper

½ tsp whole caraway seeds

½ tsp whole cumin seeds (or ¼ tsp ground)

½ tsp whole fennel seeds

1 tbsp fresh celery leaves

1 tbsp fresh parsley (or 1 tsp dried)

1 tbsp fresh sage (or 1 tsp dried)

1 tbsp fresh mint (or 1 tsp dried)

1 tbsp fresh thyme (or 1 tsp dried)

Put all the ingredients into a pan and warm very gently until just beginning to steam. Transfer to a large heat-proof jar (a Kilner jar or similar) and seal immediately. Leave to steep in a dark place at room temperature for around a week. Strain through a fine muslin and leave for another day or two. Strain again through a coffee filter, and bottle your own medieval cure-all.

The practice of distillation came to these shores when some French monks who knew the method founded monasteries in England. The first monasteries gave birth to further 'daughter' houses, and soon distilling monks had spread right across the country and out into Scotland, Wales and Ireland. The earliest definite record of spirit distilling in Britain is the order for the purchase of a still (*stillatorium*) for 12d in the year 1355, for the Infirmarius of the Benedictine monastery at Durham. Distillation had finally arrived in Britain.

Once spirits were available as a medicine it didn't take too long for the population to discover their other uses. Ireland had the honour of being the first part of the British Isles to record a death from drinking too much spirit. Richard MacRaghnaill, heir to a chieftaincy, was laid to rest after drinking uisce-betha (water of life) to excess in 1405. It's also still held by locals that the thirteen monasteries built around the Mull of Kintyre were later replaced by thirteen distilleries.

The aristocracy of all of England, Scotland, Wales and Ireland were among the first to adopt the practice of drinking spirits and have not quit it to this day. Later they would constantly condemn the habit in the general population while continuing to import the finest brandy for themselves. King Henry VI was recorded as having his own distiller in his household as early as the 1430s, joining a staff that already included an ale brewer, a beer brewer and a yeoman of the cellar.

Aqua vitae was originally distilled from wine, which was imported and expensive, but it was soon discovered that fine spirits could also be made from the cereal crops that were grown locally. The earliest record of this is of some malted barley that was granted to Friar John Cor to make aqua vitae in the Scottish Exchequer of the Rolls in 1494. This was the first step towards making whisky as we know it now, and in Scotland it was available in four different strengths: usquebaug (twice distilled), testarig (three times distilled) and usquebaug baul (four times distilled and reputedly so strong that two spoonfuls could endanger a man's life).

In Scotland as well as in Ireland they were well on the way to a pure distilled whisky, a national drink they could be proud of. In England it was more common to flavour the spirits in the same way as described in the composite or perfect aqua vitae recipes, but adapting the recipes to the locally available herbs. A mish-mash of different regional and personal recipes existed, with no particular flavour leading the pack to become England's national drink. England wouldn't find a national spirit for another 200 years.

ENGLISH AQUA VITAE: THE ORIGINAL

One recorded recipe for a compound spirit reads:

A handful each of wormwood, the tenderness of bay leaves, radish, chervil, southernwood, rue, penny-royal and other herbs; a handful and a half of liverwort and maidenhair; two handfuls of sowthistle, and three of hartstongue fern all went into the still-base, crushed and mingled together . . . and for every pottle [quart] that ye stylle, put among your herbs and wine aqua vitae of anise, and fennel and cumin.

Many of these herbs, once common, have fallen so much out of favour that they are almost entirely unknown, and many recipes are now impossible to recreate without a specialist garden. However, this anonymous recipe from 1420 uses much more familiar herbs, providing a taste of just one of the huge variety of different recipes:

Sage, fennel-roots, parsley-roots, rosemary, thyme and lavender of every each a like much.

From the notebook of William Worcester, as told to him by Brother John Wellys (c. 1860–70)

THE ALCHEMIST'S VERSION

2 tbsp fresh sage (or 2 tsp dried)
1 x 5cm cube of fennel, finely grated
2 tbsp fresh parsley roots (or finely diced celery)
1 tbsp fresh thyme (or 1 tsp dried)
2 tbsp fresh lavender (or 2 tsp dried)
300ml vodka

In a large mixing bowl, crush the herbs into the vodka using the end of a rolling pin (as if you were making a giant mojito), then transfer the whole into a jar. Seal and leave to infuse at room temperature for two days before straining through fine muslin and bottling.

The practice of distillation finally and truly passed into the secular realm with the dissolution of the monasteries in 1560. With no other means of supporting themselves, the monks who had been thrown out of the monasteries seized by the crown had to turn to whatever commercial skills they had. Many took up positions as private chaplains, tutors or clerks, while others used their medical skills to set up as apothecaries and distillers.

Around the same time it began to be fashionable for the country houses of the rich to have their stills, which many had owned previously but used only to make non-alcoholic herbal waters, turned to the task of making aqua vitae. With home-distillers dabbling in making things to their own taste, the recipes were as varied as cake recipes. They were typically used for the flimsiest of medical reasons – one recipe, credited to a John Partridge, was intended to aid the digestion, but bears a striking resemblance to absinthe, right down to the wormwood and aniseed. Another simply made a 'speedy drink which travellers may make for themselves when they are distressed for want of good beer or ale at their inn', and could make a good case for being the first recorded cocktail.

A TRAVELLER'S DRINK: THE ORIGINAL

Take a quart of good water, put thereto five or six spoonfuls of good Aqua composita which is strong of the aniseeds, and an ounce of sugar with a branch of rosemary, brew [pour] them a pretty while out of one pot into another, and there is your drink prepared. Or if you leave out the sugar it will be pleasing enough.

Hugh Plat, Sundrie New and Artificiall Remedies against Famine *(1596)*

THE ALCHEMIST'S VERSION

1 sprig fresh rosemary

100ml water

50ml sambuca (or absinthe for the brave)

2 tsp sugar

Lightly bruise the rosemary by rolling it between your hands. Add it, and all the other ingredients, to a pint glass, or one half of a cocktail shaker. Take a second pint glass, or the other half of your shaker, and pour the whole drink swiftly from one to the other. Repeat this action for 3–5 minutes, or until your arms are tired, then strain into a glass.

Drink to recover from the strain of mixing it. For true authenticity, save yourself the strain and have your valet make it.

Other flavourings for various supposed medicinal uses abounded: cinnamon or black cherry against fainting or swooning; clary to revive the heart and strengthen the back; saffron for smallpox or ague. Less pleasant were 'cordial waters', as they were known, which used animal ingredients. Cockwater used the body of a healthy young cockerel in amongst the herbs and spices of the still, to try to pass on his vitality. Snailwater was made with fresh garden snail, angelica, rosemary and cloves, and was said to protect against jaundice. The recipe then added that it would benefit even more with the addition of a quart of earthworms.

Meanwhile, amongst the poor, the drinking of simple (raw) spirits as a pick-me-up was beginning to take off in earnest. But it is in 1643 that the story of illicit spirits finally begins, with the introduction of excise duty.

Excise was created by the Long Parliament during the civil war to raise funds for the fight against the king (although when the monarchy was eventually re-established, they were more than happy to keep it in place). The excise was unique in being the first ever tax on goods produced in Britain for domestic sale, and it was just as uniquely hated. Although it later grew to encompass a huge range of goods, including meat, salt, hats, paper and tobacco, it began with only five: beer, ale, cider, soap and strong waters (spirits). Only with the introduction of a tax to be avoided did the divide begin between spirits that were produced legally under the eyes of the excise men and those which had to be produced furtively, secretly, illicitly; a divide which has now been a constant source of comedy and tragedy for almost 400 years.

CHAPTER TWO

THEY'LL NEVER TAKE OUR WHISKY

The argument over whether the Scots or the Irish were the first to invent whisky has raged for generations. I'm definitely not about to take sides, but I do know that the honour of making the first illicit whisky goes to Scotland. The reason that illicit distilling got an earlier start in Scotland is simple: the Scottish were the first to have excise imposed on them by the dastardly English government.

Excise duty was introduced in England in 1643 and was the first ever tax on home-produced goods. The introduction of the law caused an outrage (which may be difficult to imagine in an age when 20 per cent VAT has become the norm), but despite the anger there was little practical resistance. When the excise was expanded to cover Scotland in 1644, the reception was definitely no warmer. However, the excise had little effect on drinking, since the law only covered spirits produced for sale and not those made for home consumption. Making your own was far more popular. Beer and ale also remained more popular than whisky and were still untaxed. It was not until the introduction of the Malt Tax in 1713 that things really started to get serious.

Malt is grain that has been partially germinated and then dried and heated. The process turns starches in the grain, which are only good for eating, into sugars, which can be brewed into alcohol. Malted grain was used to make whisky, but more importantly – if anything can be more important than whisky – it was used to make beer. The price of beer had gone up overnight and there was literally rioting in the streets. In Glasgow a mob destroyed the house of their local MP, stealing his furniture and drinking all the wines in his cellar before setting the place alight.

Despite the riots, the tax remained in place and so people started turning their hands from resistance to evasion. Because malting grain efficiently required an extremely large, flat surface that could be heated, about the size of a barn, it was unusual for people to make their own malt. Instead professional maltsters would buy grain and malt it for sale, or they would charge a small fee for people to bring their own grain to be malted, much like a miller grinding flour. With the introduction of the tax people started malting their own grain in secret, using the spaces under their floors or in attics to produce a small batch at a time. With only small spaces available and less control over heating it was a slow and labour intensive process but at least it was tax free. They also started turning to whisky over beer, as it was much easier to smuggle a bottle of illicitly produced whisky than it was a keg of beer. All of which means that, in a way, whisky only became the Scottish national drink because of the tax imposed by the English. Hating the English has always been an important part of the Scottish national identity.

We know about the activities of illicit distillers (or smugglers, as they were known whether they were moving goods around or not) mostly from stories passed down through the generations as folk tales and local legends. So while the practice certainly started much earlier and then became widespread with the introduction of the Malt Tax, most of the accounts that have survived happened somewhat later. The reason the later tales were the ones to survive is that distilling in your bothy, quiet and undisturbed, was not much of a story. You were unlikely to be in much danger of getting caught, even though you were breaking the law and evading the tax, as enforcement was fairly lax in the first years. Excise men concentrated on raising revenue from large commercial operations rather than chasing down small family concerns. But that changed dramatically in 1781 when home distillation was not just taxed, but outlawed altogether.

During the next few years the excise men, known as 'gaugers' for the sticks they used to gauge the fullness of barrels, were given more and more powers to fine distillers – and to seize their stills, spirit, ingredients and eventually even their horses and carts, if they were used in the practice. With the introduction of fines to be collected, the officers were now motivated to actually go out and try to catch small distillers. The new laws, and the new approach to enforcement, gave the tales a villain to go up against the plucky smuggler. Plenty of good stories came about from this battle of wits between smugglers and gaugers, and a good story will always endure.

While the law continued to change over the years, with taxes going up and down and the popularity of illicit distilling with them, the basic method of distillation, of hiding and the shape of the story, became set in those years and they stayed the same for generations. Parents passed their knowledge, equipment and hiding places down to their children to carry on the family business. The practice of illicit distilling up in the glens only really died out in the 1940s. Some would say that it still hasn't – it's just that no one will tell the stories while the distillers are still alive to be caught.

The practice of distilling whisky was fairly simple. First the grain was malted by soaking it for two to three days, which could easily be done in a pond or a dammed brook. Easily but not subtly, as damming a brook was a fairly distinctive sign and one that excise officers would be looking out for; but there were ways of hiding it. One group in Loch Broom came up with a particularly ingenious method of hiding the pool they had made. They covered the pool over with planks and those with turf, then they herded a whole flock of sheep onto the top to graze. We can only hope that not too much of the sheep's waste made it down into the grain.

Once the grain began to grow shoots, which showed that the starch had been converted into sugars, then it needed to be air-dried. This was one of the riskiest stages of producing your own malt. A large, flat area under good cover was needed to spread the grain out to air-dry, and it needed to be turned regularly until the grain began to sprout. Both the space needed and the regular tending could pose a problem for smugglers. Once the grain was dry it could be taken up and heated in a kiln or over a fire to stop the sprouting and get it ready for use. The crude, smoky peat fire, which was common in illegal operations, gave the finished whisky a very strong smoked flavour and also one of its nicknames: peetreek.

Next it was time to make the wash by grinding the malt and then soaking it in hot water to draw out the sugars. The sugary water, called the wort, was drawn off and the ground malt would be soaked one or two more times to draw out all of the sugars. The leftover solids, called draff, were another sign the gaugers would be looking out for, but they were fairly simple to get rid of if there were animals around to eat them, providing no one arrived before they were finished.

All the wort could then be stored in big wash tubs, and after yeast was added it sat for a few days to ferment. The end result of all this was basically a tub of really rubbish beer that contained around 5 per cent alcohol. It was possible to just give up and drink it at this stage – although not very pleasant – and 'wash drinkers' were considered the lowest and meanest type of criminal. They were often a problem in legal distilleries, where the whisky would be well protected but the wash wouldn't, so there was always a chance of it being drunk by distillery workers or even by nocturnal visitors.

One wash drinker who lived near the Bowmore distillery in the 1960s was known as Fat Sam. He discovered that at low tide and with a bit of wading it was possible to get over the sea wall and into the distillery. He couldn't get into the spirit stores, which were locked, but he could get to the wash tuns. So he would drink wash all night and climb back over the wall before morning. One night, however, he passed out and only woke up in the morning just before the resident excise officer came in to do some morning checks. Sam staggered out of the tun room and tried to make it back over the sea wall, but he was an 18-stone man with a hangover and the tide had come in overnight. He soon found himself in serious trouble. The gauger had to come out to rescue Sam from drowning; he must have looked a pathetic picture because despite what he had been up to, the officer gave him a dram to help him recover and then simply sent him on his way. He probably thought that half-drowning was enough to teach Fat Sam a lesson by itself.

Perhaps, despite this cautionary tale, you would still like a taste of wash yourself? Just to get an idea of the experience. Making your own at home is fairly easy and while the taste isn't great, the smell is fantastic, so it's fun to do just to make your house smell like a whisky distillery.

WASH: THE ORIGINAL

The mash-tun was a cask hooped with wood, at the bottom of which, next the chime, was a hole plugged with tow. This vessel had no false bottom; in place of it, the bottom was strewed with young heath; and over this, a stratum of oat-husks. Here the mash of hot water and ground malt was occasionally mixed up for two hours; after which time the vent at bottom was opened, and the worts were allowed to filter through the stratum of oat-husks and heath. The mashing with hot water on the same grains was then repeated, and the worts were again withdrawn. The two worts being mixed in another cask, some yeast was added, and the fermentation allowed to proceed until it fell spontaneously, which happened in about three days.

Alfred Barnard, The Whisky Distilleries of the United Kingdom *(1887)*

THE ALCHEMIST'S VERSION

Ingredients:
1kg ground malt
1 packet brewer's yeast
A lot of water

Equipment:

Mash tun and wash tub (a large soup pan is ideal for the mash tun and a fermenting tub from a home brew store is best for the wash tub, but you can use another large soup pan for that too)

Thermometer

Large cheesecloth or jelly bag

String

Frame for hanging the bag (anything taller than the tub will work; a camping table is ideal, or a strong clothes horse, or even a stick resting on the backs of two chairs with weights on the seats)

Heat 3 litres of water to 65°C in the 'mash tun' pan and add the crushed malt. Hold the mixture at 65°C for half an hour using a very low heat on the stove, or heating in short bursts if your stove is too hot to hold the low temperature, and stir regularly. Stretch the cheesecloth or jelly bag over the top of your wash tub and pour the mash through it, then bunch up the opening, tie it with string and suspend it over the tub until it stops dripping. Once the first batch has dripped through, heat 2 litres of fresh water in your mash tun to 75°C and return the malt to it for a second washing. Do exactly the same as you did for the first washing but hold it at 75°C this time. The second wash can go straight in with the first. All your liquid is now 'wash'. Activate the yeast following the instructions on the packet and add it to your wash. Put the lid on loosely (some gas will need to escape, and if you seal it tightly it may explode) and leave in a warm place for 2–3 days or until the wash stops foaming.

It's ready to drink! Try not to drown in the sea. Once you've had a try you could also add some hop extract at this point to make some not entirely terrible beer.

Once the wash had finished fermenting, it was time for the smugglers to distil it at last. Many stills were fashioned by the smugglers themselves out of milk churns, old boilers or whatever else came to hand, but there were also a few firms of coppersmiths who became well known for turning out rather more stills than were necessary for the licensed distillers of the area. One in particular, Robert Armour in Campbeltown, surprisingly kept meticulous records of the illicit stills he made under the cover of a legitimate plumbing supplies business. His records have since come to light and they cover the period from May 1811, when the business was founded, to September 1817. There is no reason to believe that he stopped making stills at the end of this period – the business remained running and in family hands until 1945 – but perhaps he realised that it was ill-advised to keep a written record of his side business or perhaps the remainder of his records have been lost. The books that survive show that a complete still and condenser could be purchased for £5, a large but not impossible sum, and also that they were most often purchased by groups. Distilling was generally a community affair.

Even if they weren't operating the still as a cooperative, communities generally worked together to keep local distillers hidden from the prying eyes of the gaugers. Lots of different signals were used to warn of the approach of the excise men: washing appearing on a certain disused washing line, beacons lit on the top of hills. In one case the bothy was even built beneath a rookery, so that the rooks would be disturbed and give warning if anyone approached. The smugglers in question later turned legitimate and the rookery can still be seen just outside the Glendronach distillery.

Another favourite trick was to use a decoy when the gaugers approached. As they came towards a town they would see a young boy go running off into the moors, as if to try to warn some local smugglers. The gaugers would give chase, but the boy was only running to get them to follow and to give someone else the time to quietly go and give the real warning. He would lead the gaugers on a merry chase until they grew too tired to chase him any further or until they realised that they had been tricked, but by that point it was too late.

David Ogilvie, a well-known distiller born in 1796, was interviewed by the *Dundee Times* when he was in his nineties, and he told them about a similar incident from his younger days, when the gaugers came uncomfortably close to his bothy. As they were too close for him to make an escape, he sent his assistant up out of the bothy with a sack of pots and pans. The boy set the sack on his back and ran off across the glen, giving a metallic clattering and banging as if he were carrying the still. The gaugers gave chase, leaving Ogilvie with plenty of time to pack up the real still and get it well hidden. When the gaugers eventually lost the boy and returned, exhausted, to their horses, they found the sack sitting by them with its real contents revealed. They must have been mad as hell, but even if they had returned to the location of the bothy there would have been nothing left to find.

Fast decoys were helpful, but you could also have a good decoy that did not move at all. Because a bothy needed a good source of running water to cool the worm, as the long, coiled copper pipe used to condense the spirit was known, one of the signs of a hidden bothy that gaugers would look for was a diverted water course. So on the cliffs of Islay some smugglers diverted a stream into a sea cave, making the diversion look badly hidden. The cave they chose was high up in a cliff and completely inaccessible – no one had ever gone into it and no one ever needed to. The local excise officers spotted the diversion and spent weeks looking for a way into the cave, absolutely convinced that there must be distilling going on in there, if they could only find the secret entrance that the smugglers were using. In the meantime, they weren't keeping a vigilant eye on the rest of the area – giving all of the locals some much-needed peace for their real operations, as well as a good laugh at the officer who was hopelessly trying to climb a sheer sea cliff.

Decoys could be useful in moving whisky around as well. One group of smugglers needed to move theirs along the shore of Loch Ness to Inverness but heard that the local excise officers had got wind of their plan. So they filled a boat with casks and rowed it along the shore, looking suspicious and secretive. The excise pounced, and the smugglers pulled out cutlasses and defended their cargo violently. After a long battle they submitted to capture, only for the officers to find that the casks were all full of herring. The boat had been sent as a distraction while the whisky was moved safely overland. The boat defenders were sent to trial, but although their intentions were now obvious, there was no proof of any smuggling and the magistrate had no choice but to acquit them.

After a cold night on the seas, a day in jail and their eventual victory in court, the Loch Ness smugglers would have needed a victory dram to warm them up. A toddy would have been just the thing – but what kind? Any hot whisky drink can call itself a toddy, whatever its other ingredients, but this traditional milk toddy would have been particularly fortifying. Especially if they had been subjected to prison food during their stay.

MILK TODDY: THE ORIGINAL

A rummer tumbler, hot-water jug, milk-jug, sugar-bowl, and whisky-bottle, with sufficient wine glasses, were placed on the table. My father put just one glass of 'mountain dew' into the rummer, then sugar, then one toddy ladleful of milk. Though the 'dew' would be course and fiery, its toddy was essentially mild as cream; only nowadays I would advise drinking the milk without the 'dew'.

Osgood Mackenzie, A Hundred Years in the Highlands (1921)

THE ALCHEMIST'S VERSION

Ingredients (per glass):
50ml whisky
1 tsp sugar
100ml whole milk
Hot water to taste

Set all the ingredients out on the table, enough for yourself and for any friends who are joining you. Take your glass — a rounded wine glass is the closest you'll find to a rummer tumbler, but you can use a mug if you prefer — and measure a good double of whisky into it. Add a teaspoon of sugar and give it a good stir until the sugar begins to dissolve. Now add the milk and top the glass up with hot water until it is nearly full. Continue stirring until the sugar is fully dissolved.

Now prop your feet up by the fire, sit back and warm yourself inside and out as you contemplate how well you outwitted the law today.

When the bothy wasn't running, the still and produce would normally be moved and hidden somewhere even more secretive. Many distillers buried theirs out on the moors but in wild and shifting landscapes there was a real danger of losing track of its location. Long-forgotten casks and stashes of bottles are still discovered from time to time. It may even have been the process of sometimes losing casks and finding them again years later that led to the discovery of the benefits of oak ageing.

There were other dangers to hidden equipment. One group of distillers kept their casks of whisky and their equipment hidden in the cliffs behind the Linn-ma-Gray waterfall near Kinnaird Castle, between Perth and Aberdeen. They were lying low for the spring, having been warned that the local excise men were getting suspicious, but disaster struck when the spring thaw brought too much melt water down off the mountain. The swollen waterfall washed the still, equipment and all the casks of whisky out of their hiding place and swept them downstream to be smashed to pieces on the rocks.

Instead of using wild and out of the way places, with a little ingenuity and a lot of vigilance distillers could hide stills in plain sight where they wouldn't be lost or damaged. But it took a quick wit to manage it. Donald Macpherson was just the right kind of quick wit, and was so well known in Speyside that an account of his life, pieced together and dramatised from local tales, was serialised in a local newspaper in the 1920s.

Donald lived on a farm with his wife Janet, who would go out every day to the wash house. She would do laundry in big wooden tubs or boil up turnips for the cows in a big copper that sat in the corner of the wash house on a brick hearth. But both the tubs and the copper could be turned to another purpose when the need arose. Also the corner, covered up by a pile of peat bricks, was the entrance to a tunnel that ran underneath the hill to the back of the wash house and out into a large cave.

Down in the secret smuggler's cave the wash-backs bubbled away, fermenting ready for use. A curled copper pipe, the essential worm, also stood in the barrel of water, with one end ready to drip into a waiting cask and the other snaking back up the tunnel to emerge through a small hole near the big turnip copper. The turnip copper was actually the bottom half of a still. The top half was stored in the cave and could be placed on top and sealed to the copper with clay, then attached to the pipe running down from the hole in the wall. Once constructed, the couple had an excellent, large-capacity still that could be very quickly disassembled and hidden in times of need. The wash tubs were perfect for mashing the malt. A fine set-up, indeed.

It wasn't that the local excise officers didn't suspect the couple, just that they could never prove anything; and the Macphersons seemed to take a special joy in outwitting the gaugers so thoroughly that the gaugers ended up paying them. On one occasion they decided to raid the wash house on a day when they were certain that distilling was taking place – and it was – but, after seeing the gaugers approaching from a distance, Janet had time to fill all the wash tubs in the house with water from the cesspool and to sprinkle some pieces of cotton waste with pepper. Just before the excise men entered, she tossed some burning peats into the tubs and set the cotton waste smouldering in the corners. Waiting by the door, she slammed it shut as soon as they came in and trapped them in a room filled with foul-smelling, acrid smoke. She let them suffer for a while, stumbling in the dark trying to find the door, before opening it and scolding them for letting it shut behind them. They exited, having gained only bruised shins and burning eyes for their trouble. A few days later Donald put in a complaint with the local office about the damage caused by the unwarranted and violent search. Since they had indeed found nothing, they were forced to apologise to him.

He got even more than an apology when he was bringing malt back from the local mill and came across a pair of gaugers. He had the malt slung across the back of a pony, with a second sack of plain oatmeal on top to disguise it, when he found the pair lying in wait for him by a bridge near his home. Knowing that his pony had a bad temper, he got it to kick out at the first officer who approached it to check the sacks. As the second officer was helping his fallen colleague, Donald slipped the sack of malt over the top of the bridge and loosened the neck of the meal sack. Then he complained that the officer had upset his pony and spilt his meal all over the road. The officers searched the pony successfully this time but found no malt and, faced with the righteous anger of Mr Macpherson, they were not only unable to arrest him but actually had to give him a credit note for a replacement sack of meal at their expense. Donald returned home triumphant with the half sack of meal, a note for a new one, and the sack of malt, which he had collected from the bank beneath the bridge once the officers had gone.

The oatmeal that he'd won from the gaugers may not have been much good to distil into whisky, but it could be very good mixed with it to make the traditional drink Atholl brose. When looking for a good recipe you'll find that there are as many variations of Atholl brose as there are Highlanders. To make matters worse, the only recorded recipes tend to be in the diaries of confused English tourists. But one thing on which every recipe agrees is the need for whisky and good heather honey.

The name comes from an old tale about the Duke of Atholl, who supposedly filled the well near a rebel leader's camp with whisky, oatmeal and honey to make him too drunk to fight, although there's no evidence that the story has any basis in truth. The name also comes from the mixture of oats and water that was carried as a drink by shepherds and was called brose, even though some modern versions choose to skip the creamy oatmeal in favour of rich dairy cream. In every version the Atholl brose is beaten to a froth and sometimes eggs are added to hold the froth a little better. I have tried to combine a little of all of these to make my own version.

ATHOLL BROSE: THE ORIGINAL

Athol–brose — A compound highland drink. Sometimes, merely honey and whiskey; at others, honey, whiskey, oat–meal, and new milk.

Major Walter Campbell, The Old Forest Ranger (1850)

THE ALCHEMIST'S VERSION

50g rolled oats
350ml water
3 tbsp heather honey
2 egg yolks
250ml single cream
350ml whisky

Prepare the brose in advance by mixing the oats and water and leaving to stand overnight. In the morning, strain this with a cheesecloth or by pressing the liquid through a sieve with the back of a spoon. Beat the honey with the egg yolks in the bottom of a jug until pale and then mix in the cream. Add the brose and the whisky and whisk everything together until you have a good head of foam.

Queen Victoria was apparently fond of Atholl brose, and when she visited Atholl Castle she drank hers from a glass that had once belonged to the famous fiddler Niel Gow. So try to drink yours from a glass that once belonged to someone famous if you want to play queen.

From the stories of the Macphersons it seems that Janet was the one who did most of the work of distilling, while Donald fetched the malt and did the shouting. Indeed, while most of the surviving folk stories of daring smugglers are about men, there is little doubt that distilling was often the occupation of women. It was an ideal way for a widowed or otherwise unattached woman to make a living, and in fact the first ever conviction for illicit distilling was of a woman in Edinburgh named Bessie Campbell.

Life for an unmarried woman was hard everywhere, but especially so in the Highlands, with few occupations open to them; and worse, independent women ran the risk of being accused of witchcraft. One woman, known as Sarah of the Bog, was said to have put this reputation to good use by using it as a cover for her illicit distilling activities in the Knapdale area near Kintyre. She was even given gifts of grain and peat from her neighbours in return for putting in a good word for them with the devil; although perhaps she was actually helping them commune with more earthly spirits. In the end, the story concludes, she died when she drank too much of her own wares, fell into her fire and burned to death. Burning to death was a common motif in stories of women who got too involved with spirits. Society was sadly opposed to women gaining the independence this work could bring and such tales were told to discourage them from entering the business. The folklore was kinder, though, to women who merely worked in partnership with their husbands or who stuck to the transporting part of smuggling. In these tales, we see shades of the brave women who existed but have been largely forgotten.

Many stories about hiding whisky or stills from an unexpected inspection involve a woman as accomplice. One from the Isle of Pabbay, near Harris, involves a particularly lively female accomplice. It tells of a couple who were busy bottling whisky at home when the gaugers arrived. The woman immediately leapt into bed, beginning to moan and cry. Her husband ran out to meet the gaugers, telling them that he was so pleased that they had arrived, for his wife had just gone into labour. Would they wait with her while he ran to fetch a midwife? Hearing the noise coming from inside they decided that they would prefer to fetch the midwife themselves while he waited, giving him plenty of time to hide the whisky away before they returned with the midwife. They returned to find the woman much calmer, but were still forced to leave the family to finish the 'birth'. The midwife was no doubt a friend who left with a freshly delivered bottle for her trouble.

Another tale, from the Isle of Mull, tells of a man and his wife who were waiting for a boat to come and collect two casks, when a party of gaugers were spotted coming ashore. The husband was on the roof working on the thatch and so he saw them with some time to spare. The house was of an old design, with a fire in the middle of the room and a hole above it for the smoke to go out. There was also a chain suspended from the roof for lifting the pot on and off the fire. One keg went on the chain and was hoisted up to the roof. Then they blocked the hole in the roof so that the keg was covered up with smoke. Meanwhile, the wife grabbed the other keg and cradled it on the bed against the wall, all covered with a blanket. When the gaugers came in she crooned gently to it while she hissed at them that they could search where they liked but if they woke her baby, who was teething and had just got to sleep, then she would take the tongs to them.

The whisky-baby trick was a common story all over the country, with the 'babies' variously rocking in cradles or in bed with their mothers, often sick or newborn. At other times it is the wife, who has recently given birth, who can't be disturbed. But another tale takes us to the other end of the age spectrum, with an old woman who was alone in the house with a large keg when the gaugers came while her sons were out working the still. She tipped the keg up onto its end in front of the fire and sat on it, covering it up with her voluminous skirts. Then she took up her knitting and called for the officers to come on in. While they searched the house she apologised for not getting up, but her rheumatism was giving her terrible trouble. Respectful of their elders, they didn't disturb her, and found nothing at all in the rest of the house.

Although she clearly wasn't as frail as she pretended, she still might have taken a dram of Auld Man's Milk to celebrate her victory over the gaugers. This wonderfully rich mixture was supposed to be especially fortifying for the old. Perhaps taking it was even the reason that she was so spry.

AULD MAN'S MILK: THE ORIGINAL

Auld Man's Milk is made by beating the yolks and whites of half a dozen eggs separately. Add to the yolks sugar and a quart of milk (or thin cream), add to this about half a pint of whisky. The whipped whites are then united with this mixture and the whole is gently stirred in a punch bowl. Flavoured with nutmeg or lemon zest, this makes an admirable morning dram.

Aeneas MacDonald, Whisky *(1930)*

THE ALCHEMIST'S VERSION

2 eggs

100g caster sugar

300ml single cream

100ml whisky

Zest of ½ a lemon and/or a pinch of grated nutmeg

Separate the two eggs and whisk the whites to soft peaks in a small bowl. In a larger bowl or a jug beat the yolks, gradually adding the sugar until they are a pale yellow colour. Slowly add the cream to the yolks, beating constantly, and then do the same with the whisky. Add the lemon and/or nutmeg and mix thoroughly before gently folding in the egg whites a little at a time to leave a light, frothy and incredibly rich concoction.

Drink while feigning extreme frailty, to justify drinking an entire pot of cream.

The only relatives who were more useful to smugglers than the old and the young were the dead – although, just like the whisky babies, they didn't need to be real. Coffins were a popular transport for smuggling. One coffin was put to good use by a smuggler, Sandy, who was friends with an excise officer. Because they were friends, the officer was normally happy to turn a blind eye to his activities. However, one day Sandy decided to place a bet with him. Sandy gave the officer the name of the road that he would be bringing his whisky down that day and told him that it would be brought sometime between 9 a.m. and 5 p.m.

Determined to prove himself smarter than his friend, the officer brought his men down to the road and set them to search every cart as it went past. In the mid-afternoon, after a tiring morning of searching carts and sticking forks into every bale of hay and sack of grain, they saw a funeral procession draw near. It was travelling slowly and a long line of carts had built up behind it. Just as the hearse was approaching, one cart in the line nipped out and tried to overtake at speed. The whisky! The excise men were certain that it was Sandy trying to get away and they gave chase – but when they caught up they found nothing but turnips and returned to their posts to search fruitlessly for the rest of the day. That evening, in the pub, the officer was angry with Sandy for trying to trick him. He was certain that nothing could have got past him and that Sandy must have cheated and taken his whisky by another route, keeping him distracted to boot. 'I kept my word,' said Sandy, 'and you saw it for yourself. I know you saw it, you took your hat off to it!'

An Edinburgh city official, Archie Campbell, also made use of the respect given to hearses when he was taking his mother's body up to her Highland birthplace for burial. The hearse went up full of body and came back full of whisky. He was heard to say, 'I took away the mortal remains but brought back the spirit.'

The dead were as useful in the house as they were on the road. John Monroe ran a ship's chandlers in Ross-shire, which was a handy cover for a little distilling and distribution on the side. One day he had a large quantity of whisky waiting in his cellar to be loaded onto a ship to Inverness, when he heard that there were some particularly nosy gaugers in the area. He persuaded a visiting tailor to help him out in exchange for a boll of malt (enough to make some 250 pints of whisky). The tailor lay down on top of the trap door to the cellar, covered in a sheet, to play dead. When the officers saw that the household was in mourning for poor Monroe's brother, they respectfully left – although the plan had nearly been blown just as the gaugers entered, when the tailor demanded a second boll of malt or he would give the game away. He left with his two bolls and the gaugers found out too late that John Monroe had no brother.

Even the clergy conspired with the smugglers – or sometimes did more than just conspire with them. In Orkney there was a church officer by the name of Magnus Eunson who did a little smuggling of his own, and liked to keep his whisky hidden in the pulpit. Whenever there were excise officers in attendance at the church he would denounce the evils of drink with a great fervour, while being careful not to clink with his feet. Some new arrivals suspected his involvement, but Magnus was tipped off by one of his parishioners about a search they were planning to make of the church. He had time to move all the whisky and paraphernalia to his home, where he stowed most of it under the dining table and the rest on top, with a coffin lid balanced on the top of that. Finally the table and 'coffin' were all covered over with a large white sheet and the church officer and his household servants gathered around it in poses of mourning, starting up a dramatic lament. The officers came to the door and made to come in, obviously still suspicious; but when an attendant took them aside and whispered to them that the man had died of smallpox, they decided a search was not worth the risk, and quickly left.

Most stills were only used to produce whisky for the distillers and perhaps their immediate friends and neighbours. But for those who wanted to sell it for cash, the whisky had to be skilfully moved, and their biggest market was in the towns. Towns were busy and carefully watched, unlike the smuggler's home glens, so it was the last mile that was the most difficult part of the journey. This meant it was often easier to sell the whisky on the outskirts, to more specialist smugglers.

Near Dundee was a village called Auchterhouse, where the inhabitants specialised in smuggling into the city. Producers would bring their whisky to the town in casks, where it was transferred to bladders that could be hidden underneath clothes by the locals, who would look much less suspicious walking about the city than strangers. They earned themselves the name of 'bladdermen' for their trade. Women were the best smugglers, able to hide a good bladder under their voluminous skirts, but the men had their ways as well. One Geordie Fleming was known for his balancing skill and could hide a full bladder under a very tall hat, while others would use milk churns with false bottoms.

The whisky smuggled into the towns often wasn't the best stuff – the smugglers kept that for themselves – and it wasn't aged, as all whisky must be today. Add to that a trip in a bladder or a milk churn, which wouldn't do much to improve it, and you'd be getting some pretty rough stuff. The best thing to do was add some flavouring to disguise the bite. One popular treatment was to turn it into Highland bitters, which were drunk medicinally by the glass before meals – quite unlike cocktail bitters, which we only use now in tiny quantities.

HIGHLAND BITTERS: THE ORIGINAL

On the sideboard there always stood before breakfast a bottle of whisky, smuggled, of course, with plenty of camomile flowers, bitter orange peel, and juniper berries in it – 'bitters' we called it – and of this he had a wee glass always before we sat down to breakfast, as a fine stomachie.

Osgood Mackenzie, A Hundred Years in the Highlands *(1921)*

THE ALCHEMIST'S VERSION

4 tsp dried chamomile flowers or 4 chamomile teabags
Zest of 2 oranges (Seville or marmalade oranges if you can get them)
2 tbsp dried juniper berries
½ bottle of cheap whisky (the younger the better,
although anything younger than three years can't legally
be called whisky. If you want to be really authentic,
you can buy unaged whisky direct from a distillery,
but they have to call it 'new-made spirit')

*Add everything to the whisky (this will be easier with a full
size bottle which is half empty than a half size bottle so you
might want to get some help to drink the first half), and leave
it in the bottle for 2–3 weeks. Keep it on the sideboard and
strain into your glass with a tea strainer whenever you want
a dram, leaving the rest in the bottle to steep even longer.
A glass before breakfast is, apparently, excellent to settle
the stomach.*

For all their skill at concealment, things did not always go
the smugglers' way, and occasionally the excise men would
be the ones to win the battle of wits. Sometimes they even
had the help of an unwitting accomplice. Seumas Mor
McDonald was a farmer and famous distiller on the shores
of Loch Kay who had been easily outwitting the local gaugers for years, much to their frustration. One day, after
yet another fruitless search of his farm, one of the excise
officers hit upon an idea. He left the farm, went to the
nearest neighbour, John Robertson, and told him that he
had found the still. He asked Robertson to bring out his
horse and cart so that he could use it to carry the still away
to Killin. The farmer dutifully brought out his horse and
cart and led them up to the McDonald farm, then past
the gate. He stopped a little distance down the lane, and a
search of the nearby field soon revealed the bothy hidden
in a knoll by the track. Since he thought the officers had

already found the still, he hadn't considered that he might be leading them right to it.

Sometimes, though, the gaugers stumbled upon operations more through luck than judgement. Locals had been running a still inside the Dufftown clock tower for years without fear of discovery. With the smell and smoke of the large number of legitimate distilleries surrounding it, no one was ever likely to notice a little extra coming from the tower. What they hadn't bet on was a young excise officer who was a keen amateur horologist, or clock enthusiast, visiting the town. He noticed that the clock on the tower had stopped and climbed up to investigate, only to find a running still where the workings should have been.

Customers couldn't be trusted, either. A legendary smuggler known as Goshen had been safely staying ahead of the excise for years. In his old age, he would occasionally let trusted customers come and watch him work. His showing off would eventually be his downfall. Surprisingly, it was Sir William Grant, MP for Banffshire and Master of the Rolls, who was unable to keep his mouth shut. At a dinner party he told his fellow guests a story about watching the best distiller in Scotland at work. The guests all found the story very entertaining – except for a senior figure in the excise, who Grant had not realised was present. After getting the location out of Grant the officer led the raid personally and seized a still and mash tun. Luckily Goshen got away with a £10 fine, as he was quite old by this time and his lawyer did a good job of playing him up as weak and feeble. With the loss of his equipment, Goshen decided that it was time to give up the distilling game for good and stick to his legitimate trade of innkeeper. The Fiddichside Inn is still owned and run by his descendants to this day, but the whisky they serve just isn't as good as it used to be.

It wasn't only other people you had to fear: the local wildlife could cause trouble, too. One smuggler in Aultmore had his bothy destroyed when a cow fell through the roof – but at least the cow wasn't able to arrest him. John MacDonald was arrested after a gamekeeper fell through the roof of his bothy and proved a bit more talkative than a cow; MacDonald was sentenced to six weeks' imprisonment. Even arrest didn't stop some smugglers, though – he was able to come to an arrangement with his jailer, who let him out at night to go and work his bothy provided that he returned in the morning, bringing a dram for the jailer, and was safely locked up again before the day shift arrived. Since no one suspected an imprisoned man of distilling, it was the safest period of production that he ever had.

At other times, smugglers were only a whisker away from capture before the tables were turned at the last minute. In a small bay on the shores of Kinlochmoidart, a party of smugglers were working happily at a still when a group of gaugers came towards them across the sands. But the gaugers didn't know the bay well like the locals did and they walked straight into a pocket of quicksand. They begged the smugglers to help them as they sank. They did so, but only after receiving the officer's word that they would not report anything they had seen that day. Despite their luck, the smugglers still had to move their operation, knowing that bay would not be a safe place to work now that the gaugers knew the way out of the sands.

Smugglers usually liked to have a dram as they worked, but the new-made spirit, straight out of the still, would have been pretty rough stuff. Most would have drunk it neat regardless, or with a little water, but there is one traditional recipe that might have improved it. It is quick to make, and involves only a small number of ingredients, ones that wouldn't spoil and were easy to store. It could easily have been whipped up at still-side, to make the whisky that came fresh from the still a little more palatable. Since the ingredients and method are simple, I've created a version that lets you make it by the glass as a cocktail, but originally it would have been made by the bottle.

CALEDONIAN LIQUOR: THE ORIGINAL

A simpler beverage is Caledonian Liquor, which is made by dropping an ounce of oil of cinnamon on two and a half pounds of bruised loaf sugar; a gallon of whisky — the best you can lay hands on — is added to this and, when the sugar is dissolved, the liquor is filtered and bottled.

Aeneas MacDonald, Whisky (1930)

THE ALCHEMIST'S VERSION

1 sugar cube (demerara is best)
Drop of pure cinnamon oil
50ml whisky (again, the younger the better)

Just pop the sugar cube in the bottom of a tumbler, splash a drop of cinnamon oil onto it, add the whisky and stir until dissolved. Sip cautiously, keeping one eye on the still and another out for the gaugers.

A Strathtay smuggler had a close call when he was caught by gaugers while he was in his boat at a river dock, about to offload his whisky. They chased him down the river but both boats were rowboats and with more rowers, the gaugers seemed bound to catch him. He slowed down and called out that he was surrendering, then took hold of one of the officers' oars to help them aboard. It was a trick: at the last minute he grabbed the oar, pulled it up into his boat and took off at full speed. The gaugers, left with only one oar, were barely able to paddle themselves to the bank, while the smuggler was soon out of sight and able to stow the cask in a riverside hidey-hole before they had the chance to return with backup.

James McGregor had two close calls before he turned legitimate, setting up the Balmenach distillery near

Grantown-on-Spey. The gaugers first came many years earlier, when he was working in a cavern with his two brothers. The cavern was deep in the rock with only one narrow entrance, plus a small chimney to which the stove-pipe was firmly attached. The brothers were sold out by a local-turned-informant who led a team of excise officers straight down the only entrance. The cavern was completely dark except for the fire of the stove. Two of the brothers were asleep, with the other left awake to stoke the fire. The excise men were almost upon them, sneaking through the dark, when the brother who was stoking the fire opened the stove door to add another peat. He saw the gaugers creeping up on them in the flash of light and immediately disconnected the stove pipe, filling the cave with thick smoke, then he fired his pistol in the general direction of the officers. The shot scattered them, as well as waking his brothers, and in the confusion they were able to slip out. They got away – though not without the loss of their equipment, which they had to leave behind.

After this loss, two of the brothers turned to legitimate occupations. One became a miller and the other a farmer. The third brother also became a farmer, but unlike the first, he kept up his whisky distilling in a shed on his farm at Balmenach. One day the local excise officer came to the farm to pay him a visit. He looked around without much enthusiasm for the hunt, asking about the buildings, but seeming to believe the answers. He passed the hen house, the storage barns and the peat shed without stopping to look inside them. Then, with duty lightly done, they returned to the house to share a dram or two late into the evening. It was only as the officer was leaving that he turned to James McGregor and said, 'If I were you, Mr McGregor, I'd take out a licence for yon peat shed.' James soon did, and in 1824 the Balmenach distillery was officially founded.

James McGregor was not the only one turning legitimate around that time. The Excise Act of 1823 had made getting a licence easier and cheaper, rendering legitimacy more attractive than it had been in years. The danger now was less from the authorities than from your fellow smugglers, if you betrayed them by taking out a licence. The first person to do so in an area would attract an excise man, come to monitor their legal business and make life much more difficult for all their neighbours.

The Glenlivet area had been famous since the 1790s for both the high quality of its whisky and the great number of stills in the glen. It was reputed that at the height of illicit distilling in the valley, there could be up to fifty stills running at any one time. It was going to be a brave man who angered so many fellow distillers by taking the first licence. That man was George Smith, who came from a distilling family of long and excellent reputation. He took up the licence in 1823 with the encouragement and support of the local landowner, making himself not only the first distiller in the valley to do so, but the first in the whole country.

After opening the distillery, Smith was in real fear for his life. The local smugglers threatened to burn his distillery to the ground with him in it, and as a consequence of the threats he was given a gift by the local laird: a pair of hair-trigger pistols, which he wore on his belt every day for the rest of his life. These pistols are on display in the visitor centre of the Glenlivet distillery to this day. Smith also had the distillery guarded by armed men both day and night, and often personally accompanied the pack horses taking his produce down to the coast. His vigilance paid off and, while other distillers who tried to follow his lead and open legal distilleries in the glen were soon scared off, his distillery stayed open. Today, it produces the most-drunk single malt in the world.

George Smith only ever had to fire his pistols once (although the same probably could not be said of his armed guards), and when he did, it was not at smugglers but at common thieves. He had stopped in a tavern on the way home from making a large delivery, his pockets bulging with the proceeds. The innkeeper showed him into a back room where a number of large, disreputable-looking men were waiting to have some profitable words with any rich travellers who came through. George drew one of his pistols and fired it into the hearth, spraying burning fragments of peat across the floor. The men thought better of choosing him as a target, and quietly left him to his drink.

The violence he faced from the smugglers was very real, and while the folk tales always tell of the clever smuggler getting the best of the excise using only his wits, court records and officers' reports show that they sometimes chose a simpler solution. The violence was generally limited to threats with weapons or a beating at worst; but there were times when things would be taken to a fatal conclusion, especially if the officers had caused injury to one of their own.

Close to Inverness, a group of smugglers were hiding in a barn with the wicker door securely fastened when an excise officer ran the door through with his sword while attempting to get it open. To his surprise and horror his sword came back covered in blood – he had stabbed a smuggler who was listening close to the other side of the door. His friends, thinking that he had been killed, fell upon the officer and beat him into unconsciousness. He was carried to the nearby Bogroy Inn by his fellow officers but soon died of his injuries. The smuggler, on the other hand, survived his injury and lived to a ripe old age, showing off his scar in the inn.

The Bogroy Inn was also the scene of a more cheerful tale, according to the locals (although people on Mull will also swear that it was their local inn where this incident took place). In both cases, the story is the same. A group of gaugers who had successfully seized a cask of whisky stopped at the inn for the night, locking the cask up in their room before going downstairs for dinner. In the meantime, the original owners of the cask had been informed of the location of their whisky, and one of the staff who had helped the gaugers to carry the cask up told them exactly where in the room it stood. So the smugglers took an auger and drilled up through the floor and right up into the barrel, letting the whisky pour out into another barrel below. Then they were away with their (now slightly floor-flavoured) whisky before the gaugers even knew that it was gone.

It was often easier to retrieve spirits later than it was to prevent them from being taken in the first place. A couple of different tales are told of the Foss Inn, which must have had a very smuggler-friendly landlord. In the first story, some gaugers stopped at the inn bringing some casks of whisky that they had captured from a man called Ewan Fletcher, along with two of his ponies. While they were at the bar, a cousin-in-law of Ewan's struck up a friendly conversation with them. He offered them the hire of his cart to take the casks of whisky back to their base at Pitlochry, as the ponies would never manage to carry the casks that far by themselves. He kept them occupied with a round of drinks and offered to transfer the casks over to the cart himself while they enjoyed their dram. Meanwhile, Ewan himself had arrived, and together they swapped the casks over for casks of water so that Ewan could retrieve the whisky.

The next gaugers to arrive at the Foss Inn were warier – perhaps they had even heard about the first incident. They had seized a still and some other equipment, and they weren't letting any of it out of their sight. They ate in their room and had everything locked up in there with them when they went to sleep. But once they were soundly asleep, the smuggler, Donald, climbed down a rope from the roof and came in through the window. He retrieved his equipment, after first sneaking through the room gathering all of the gaugers' shoes and tossing them out of the window. When he finally grabbed the still and made a quick exit the men were woken by the jingling sound of the worm – as they were bound to be – but the time they wasted looking in vain for their shoes gave Donald a good head start. When they finally came down to the yard in their stockinged feet to start the pursuit, he was already long gone.

After the legitimate trade started to take off in the mid-1800s, the ways that the gaugers could be tricked changed in character a little. While there were still illicit distillers around doing things in the traditional way, there were also more stories told about liberating whisky from someone else's distillery. One of the best tricks was to take whisky that would otherwise have gone to waste, as no one was going to miss it. The wood of a whisky cask is porous – a property that allows the whisky to interact with the wood and gain all those wonderful flavours from ageing – but it also means that after the cask is emptied, the wood is left damp with whisky. In normal practice, the casks would simply be allowed to dry out and the whisky would be lost. It wasn't worthwhile for the distiller to extract that last bit when they had already bottled the rest of the barrel, but it was a fine temptation to distillery workers.

A common practice, when the supervisor's back was turned, was 'grogging' the cask by swirling water around inside it to extract some of that leftover whisky. It worked well, but left you with a very weak mix of whisky and water. Alternatively, some of the pure whisky could also be drawn out of the wood by heat. During a particularly hot summer in Cameronbridge in the 1970s, one of the distillery workers discovered that the heat of the sun was enough to draw a couple of bottles out of the wood of each cask. So he started going back every night to the storehouse where the barrels were kept, and all he had to do was turn them over and pour the whisky out. He might never have been caught if he hadn't been stupid enough to set up a stall on Livingston market selling the stolen spirit, where he was swiftly spotted by the authorities.

But what would grogged whisky taste like? It would be weak and watery due to the extraction process, but it would also be extremely strongly flavoured by the oak as it was the part of the whisky that had been deep in the wood of the barrel. I've tried to recreate that taste with a little bit of trickery so that you can get an idea of what it would have been like.

GROGGED WHISKY: THE ALCHEMIST'S VERSION

100ml whisky (you will want an aged single malt this
time, but don't go ruining anything too good, please)
2 tbsp oak chips (you can pick these up for smoking food)
100ml water

Put the whisky and the oak chips into a sealed jar for a week, shaking from time to time. Strain the chips out of the whisky with a sieve or tea-strainer and mix with an equal quantity of water.

You've made your own grogged whisky! Now drink up quick, before the foreman catches you.

In Rothes, it was the coppersmiths who were up to a little bit of no good alongside their legitimate business. A. Forsyth & Sons was an old firm, one that probably once had a sideline making smugglers' stills, but which by the 1930s was happily and profitably employed in making and maintaining stills for legal distilleries. Still, they couldn't resist every now and then helping themselves to a bit of the wash as they were working on the stills. They would take it back to the copper works and put a small still onto the furnace they normally used for working copper. The worm would go in the bucket they used to cool the worked metal. They only made a bit for themselves, doing it just because they could and because they enjoyed the cheek of doing it in the works right across the road from the excise man's house. The smell of so many nearby distilleries, and the smoke from their normal work, meant that there was little chance of getting caught – and they never were.

By the 1900s the licensed distilleries had taken hold in a serious way and smuggling was largely reduced to a hobby for a few rather than a big business; although there was a small surge in the 1920s and 1930s, when many distilleries shut down due to the war and the smugglers took over supply for a while, just until the distilleries got up and running again. On the other hand, if some stills had remained running in the burns and the glens, would they tell us? Would I tell you? It's only really safe to tell stories about a smuggler once he is already dead and gone beyond the reach of the law.

CHAPTER THREE

THE GIN CRAZE

in has become a high-class drink, an artisan product steeped in empire and favoured by tuxedoed spies. It wasn't always that way, though; far from it. When it was first introduced, gin was the drink of the poor and the destitute. It was the drink of highwaymen, outlaws and revolutionaries. It sparked a runaway moral campaign and seven years of effective prohibition. In that time there were hidden shops, riots and secret cabals of informers. Welcome to the Gin Craze.

While Scotland was beginning to develop whisky into its national spirit, in defiance of the law, the new king was about to introduce and encourage the drink that would become England's. William of Orange had become king when he overthrew James II at the invitation of the English gentry. At the time of William's invasion James had been king for only three years, since the death of his brother Charles II. Their father, Charles I, had been executed by his own Parliament, leading to twenty years of England operating as a commonwealth without a king. So William was taking the throne of a country that did not appear to have much respect for its rulers. He must have been nervous.

Instead of royalty, the people of London idolised highwaymen. The notorious Dick Turpin was out on the road and in his prime. They worshipped and celebrated the multiple prison escapee John Sheppard, who was paraded around town for fifteen days after his last escape from the heart of Newgate. They loved to hate anyone with any standing or with money, and complaints were made that no one wearing court dress could walk the streets without being harassed or pelted with mud. People everywhere drank toasts to 'the king across the water' (James II's son, the Prince of Wales) – they might not have liked him much better than William if he had turned up, but it did sound romantic, and it annoyed the government, so it made a good toast. But at least William would bring them a new pleasure that would grow and flourish. When one of his successors, George II, presided over a ban some years later, he would become more hated for it than William could have imagined.

With much to prove to his new subjects, William of Orange took the traditional approach of English kings: he declared war on France. His first act of aggression was to lay a cripplingly heavy tax on their main export: brandy. Britain had enjoyed a time of freedom and plenty since the demise of Oliver Cromwell and the end of the Commonwealth. Crops were good, food was cheap, towns were booming – and visiting brandy shops was becoming a popular pastime.

Cutting off the supply of brandy was unlikely to be a popular move. Luckily, there was an alternative: cheap spirits made from British grain, which was growing in such plenty that farmers were in need of a new market.

These native spirits were usually used to make gin, the perfect spirit for the Dutch king to promote; and so gin was to become the new national spirit of England. Steps were taken to promote the new industry. Duty was dropped to almost nothing, and the sale of spirits was entirely deregulated. In London, even bakers couldn't open a shop without going through a seven-year apprenticeship, but now anyone with a room or a wheelbarrow and a little spare cash for some cheap spirits could set themselves up as a dram shop (or dram barrow). It was one direction from the monarch that the people were happy to obey. The king said to drink cheap gin, and drink it they did!

While the poor were happy to take to the new drink, the rich weren't satisfied with cheap spirits. They still wanted French brandy, and it was smuggled in for them at great risk and expense. But for every barrel of genuine French brandy there were half a dozen counterfeits. Why take the risk on the high seas in the middle of a war, when you could knock up a fake in your shed and make a killing? Even if the fake was spotted, there was little your customers could do once you had taken their money and left. They couldn't exactly complain to the authorities that their illegal smuggled goods were fakes. The counterfeit just had to be good enough to make the sale. To make it more convincing, some counterfeiters would even load their fakes into boats in the dead of night and drop them out at sea. Then the next night, watched by their trusting customers, they would head back out and pick their cargo up as if it had been smuggled in from France.

'AUTHENTIC' NASSAU BRANDY: THE ORIGINAL

For two gallons and a half:

Take two gallons of British brandy, one in five, one pound and a half of Lisbon Sugar, six ounces and a half of prunes, four ounces of cellery, three ounces of kernels, two ounces of orange peel, a teaspoon full of essence of lemon, two glasses of rose water, and fill up your two and a half gallon cask with water.

P. Boyle, The Publican and Spirit Dealer's Daily Companion, or, plain and interesting advice to wine vault and public house keepers, On subjects of the greatest Importance to their own Welfare, and to the Health, Comfort & Satisfaction Of Their Customers & Society At Large *(Sixth Edition, c. 1800)*

THE ALCHEMIST'S VERSION

200ml vodka

Zest of ½ an orange

Zest of ¼ of a lemon

2 tsp apricot kernels
6 large prunes, roughly chopped
1 x 3cm piece of celery, sliced
1 tbsp rosewater
75ml water

Add all the ingredients except for the rosewater and the water into a large jar with a lid. Seal the jar and leave to steep for a fortnight, shaking occasionally. After a fortnight, strain through a sieve, and then strain again through a coffee–filter paper. Add a tablespoon of rosewater and 75ml of water, mix thoroughly and serve.

For real authenticity, fill your bath with salt water, seal your brandy into a small wooden cask, drop it in and leave overnight. Enjoy sipped from a brandy balloon with a fine cigar, while you think about how you got ripped off by those damn smugglers again. It's quite tasty, but not at all convincing to anyone who has ever tasted real brandy.

But if the king was promoting gin consumption, then what changed? How did it get to be an illegal substance sold in secret? The trouble started with the old Puritans kicking up trouble, perhaps pining for Cromwell's England of closed theatres, enforced fast days and banned make-up. The magistrates of Middlesex were asked to hunt out some 'scandalous clubs or societies of young persons who meet together and in the most impious and blasphemous manner insult the most sacred principles of our holy Religion, affront Almighty God himself, and corrupt the mind and morals of each other'. The clubs were pure imagination and the committee found none, but they did get the chance to make a report to the Lord Chancellor. One of their number, Sir John Gonson, took the opportunity to rail against all the evils of scandalous modern London. He hated the irreverent plays and shameless gambling houses, he hated the whores on the streets, but most of all, he hated the dram shops.

There certainly were a lot of them – the promotion of gin had been a great success. In St-Giles-in-the-Fields one house in every five sold gin, without even counting the hawkers on the street. Gin was sold not just in the dedicated dram shops, but in grocers, barbers and tobacconists. Employers would sell their workers a dram or two every day on credit, taking it straight out of their wages. An unscrupulous employer (and there were plenty of them) might leave you with no wages at all after you'd paid for your gin. The slums were already becoming the dirty, poor and miserable places that would shock the Victorians who discovered the joys of philanthropy a hundred years later. For many, gin was their only comfort and relief, and they took their comfort by the pint.

A market woman, testifying in court, had this to say about her gin: 'We market women are up early and late, and work hard for what we have. We stand all weathers, and go thro' thick and thin. It's well known, that I was never the woman that spar'd my carcass; and if I spend three farthings now and then, in such a simple stuff as we poor souls are glad to drink, it's nothing but what's my own. I get it honestly, and I don't care who knows it; for if it was not for something to cheer the spirits between whiles, and keep out the wet and cold; alackaday! it would never do! We should never be able to hold it; we should never go thorow-stitch with it, so as the keep body and soul together.' The poor had never had access to affordable spirits before, only weak beer, but they'd taken to them with enthusiasm to dull the edges of their hard lives.

Of course, politicians and reformers didn't see excessive drinking as a symptom of poverty; they saw it as the cause. Gin was nothing less than a wicked demon that had possessed the poor – and it could only be exorcised by force.

The first attempt at a ban, in 1729, was a laughable failure. Sir Robert Walpole, who was prime minister in all but name, was looking for a way to raise money to buy the love of the crown. The reformers gave him an excuse for a huge new tax, and he took it. A hastily drafted bill laid a five-shilling duty on every gallon of gin, and required retailers to buy a licence that cost more than double the average annual wage. The only concession to the livelihoods that would be destroyed was granting permission for distillers to set up in any other trade without apprenticeship.

There was one serious flaw. The bill only placed a duty on gin, not on all spirits, and not even on the base spirit used to produce gin. Spirit was produced raw by large distillers – rich gentlemen who the Parliament could not afford to upset – so it only became liable for tax when it was flavoured by one of the hundreds of small backstreet compounders, and became gin. Gin was defined by the act as a spirit flavoured with 'juniper berries, or other fruit, spices, or ingredients'. The solution was simple. The compounders, who were usually also the retailers, simply stopped flavouring it. They were so pleased with themselves for tricking the gentlemen of Parliament that they called the raw spirit 'parliamentary brandy', and sold it openly in the streets.

Parliamentary brandy certainly wasn't pleasant to drink. Imagine the worst vodka you can remember drinking. Even that roughest vodka has been filtered through charcoal at least once to remove unwanted flavours. This spirit was unfiltered, and made from the cheapest and worst grain available. But it was theirs: Parliament had not managed to take it from them, and its bitter taste was the taste of defiance.

The rough parliamentary brandy was fine for the street sellers, but publicans had more demanding customers. Luckily the new bill was made more of loopholes than of law, and gin was also untaxable if it was made into punch before it was sold. Punch was popular, and publicans had a wide range of inventions. It was a point of pride for most to have their own special and secret recipe. Some came with fruit and sugar, and weren't a long way from the modern cocktail. Others were a bit stranger – like this recipe for milk punch, intended to be particularly suitable for the sick or the young. It begins by curdling milk, which may sound disgusting, but once the solids are filtered out it's actually quite delicious.

MILK PUNCH: THE ORIGINAL

An approved method of making milk punch

For five gallons

Two gallons of spirits, otherwise brandy or rum, 1 in 5 underproof, 2 gallons of water, 1 pint of orange juice, one quart of lemon ditto, three pounds and a half of loaf sugar; fill it up with skimmed milk, and when fine, bottle it off, putting a piece of sugar-candy in each bottle.

P. Boyle, The Publican and Spirit Dealer's Daily Companion *(Sixth Edition, c. 1800)*

THE ALCHEMIST'S VERSION

4 parts gin

2 parts water

2 parts neat sugar syrup

¼ part orange juice
½ part lemon juice
1½ parts skimmed milk

Mix all the ingredients except for the milk in a jug and stir well. Now be prepared for the nasty bit: add the skimmed milk, stir again and watch it curdle. Leave the punch to settle until the solids have risen to the top, then filter it though a coffee–filter paper to leave a clear, sweet punch.

For authenticity you should drink with a plain sugar candy in each glass, but it can be hard to find them unflavoured unless you are willing to make your own. Sugar–crystal coffee stirrers make a good substitute, or try different flavours of candy to see which ones will go. Just don't try mint. Trust me, mint is terrible. I try these things so that you don't have to.

The law was an obvious failure, and it was quietly repealed in 1733. This celebratory poem, dedicated to the gin drinkers of Britain and Ireland, appeared in all the newspapers:

What can impart such solace to mankind,
As this most powerful dram, which levels all
The different ranks in this unequal world?
The poor plebeian, elevate by Gin,
Fancies himself a king.

A victory for the friends of gin! But the reformers had it in their sights now, and they weren't going to give up so easily. A year later, a story arrived in the papers that gave them the moral firepower they needed to demand that something be done. A young girl was sadly on trial for the murder of her own child. Her trial took place in a packed court, providing free entertainment to the huge portion of the population who could not read, while the upper classes were shocked by the sensational accounts that were published in all the newspapers.

Judith Defour was a single mother. She had a job, but it only paid two or three shillings a week – not nearly enough to look after her young daughter – so Mary had to live in the workhouse. One Sunday Judith came to the workhouse to take Mary out for the day, but she was told that she couldn't even see her own daughter without a note of permission from the church wardens. She went away and came back with a note, which later turned out to be forged, and took her daughter away. Later that evening she arrived at work, obviously very drunk. After persuading a friend to lend her a penny for a roll she returned with a dram of gin, tossed it back and broke down. She told her workmates that she had left her child lying in a field all night.

At the trial she said that it was a vagrant, Sukey, who persuaded her to do it. They had been drinking all afternoon, but eventually they had run out of money. She didn't understand why she agreed when Sukey suggested that they sell the new clothes that the workhouse had given to Mary.

The two women stripped her and tried to leave her in a ditch, but she would not stop crying. They tied a linen rag around her neck to quiet her, and ended up strangling her to death. The vagrant was never found. Judith had only met her that day, and did not know her surname or have any idea where she might be found. She broke down frequently in court and was devastated by the guilt of what she had done. Judith's mother testified in court that her daughter 'never was in her right mind' the whole of her life. There was surely more at work in Judith's case than gin – the poor wages that forced her to put her daughter in the workhouse even though she was working full-time, for a start – but for the reformers, the cause and the enemy were clear. Gin was the cause and nothing else.

After the popularity of the trial of Judith Defour, news-papers competed to publish the most lurid stories about the evils of gin. They wrote to shock and moralise, but also to entertain and keep their readers reading. Some of the stories were harrowing, but others were more than a little naughty. Many were probably the complete invention of desperate journalists who were paid by the article, but reformers lapped them up as they were told exactly what they wanted to hear.

There was the story of Jane Andrews, a maidservant to a Kensington brewer, which appeared in London's *Daily Post*. Her master went out of town for a few days and she went straight to her usual gin shop. It was only ten in the morning, but she had money in her pocket – a strangely large amount for a maid – and soon found willing drinking companions. After having a few drinks, and then buying a few bottles to take away, she invited a drummer, a chimney-sweep and a woman traveller back to the house. They drank together all day in the master's sitting room, staining the upholstery and leaving bottles among the mantelpiece trinkets. They drank until about four in the afternoon, when Jane suggested that they all go to bed together, and not for sleeping, on the master's fine sheets. Off with their clothes and in they hopped, and they were still enjoying themselves and each other when a mob surrounded the door and demanded they stop. The newspaper doesn't explain how the mob knew what was happening, but they soon gained entry. A closet door in the bedroom was found to have been broken in, and some of Jane's master's money taken. She was charged with theft, and the drummer, who she had thought was her friend and lover, even spoke as a witness against her at trial.

Then there was the problem of women who, if they drank too much gin, might just burst into flames. The medical theory of the four humours, which still had its adherents, said that women were cold and wet by nature. So it was thought that too much spirit – supposedly hot and dry in nature – might easily make them shrivel up and dry out until they were like tinder, ready to catch fire at any moment. More than one case of a woman who was a heavy drinker simply bursting into flames and burning to death was reported, and apparently believed. They usually burned late at night when they were alone and were only found the next morning, reduced to ash. Often a foot, a few fingers or the top of the head were left untouched as well as all the furniture around them. Sometimes the whole room was left covered in an oily soot that ruined everything it came into contact with; at other times there was nothing but a terrible smell, which soon dissipated. This idea would last a shockingly long time, too: Charles Dickens himself was a believer in the idea that drinkers might spontaneously combust.

Eventually the government had no choice but to give in to the moral outrage and draw up a new act, similar to the first but harsher and broader, with the loopholes taken out. There would be no more parliamentary brandy. No real brandy or rum, either. The act brought in a retail licence costing £50, and a duty of twenty shillings a gallon on spirits of every kind – but only, and this was the really sore point, on the sale of quantities less than two gallons. A gentleman who could afford it and was able to store it could buy a whole case of brandy for his cellar without paying any of the new duty. A poor woman buying a quartern of gin at her local dram shop, which before would only have cost her a penny, would now pay seven and a half pence for the duty alone. It was prohibition in all but name, and it was prohibition only for the poor.

The day was set for the Gin Act to come into effect – 29 September 1736 – and the government expected real political trouble. They knew that already they weren't well liked by the populace, for reasons including the clampdown on smugglers, large gifts of public money to the king and even the building of Westminster Bridge, which would wipe out the livelihoods of hundreds of Thames boatmen. Now they were taking Madam Geneva away from a volatile public as well.

At the same time, the men of Parliament lived with the constant threat that the exiled son of King James II – another James, the one poetically known as the king across the water – might return. Their terror was intensified when in June 1736 a bomb went off in Westminster Hall. It wasn't much of a bomb, just a small charge of gunpowder, tucked under a bench. Not likely to cause much injury, but it made a good bang, spreading smoke and copies of a badly printed manifesto all around the room. Two more explosions were planned, but the conspirators dropped the other parcels while running from the hall. No one was so much as injured in the blast and within a month the three conspirators were caught, tried and hung for treason; but still, Parliament was alarmed.

Then there was the Gin Plot. In the days running up to 29 September, letters were sent to distillers, gin shops and publicans claiming to be from James Stuart himself (although I'm sure he had better things to do than write personal letters to the local pub). A few copies made their way into the hands of the terrified politicians. They made vague allusions to revolution, to the support of the army and to the support of mysterious important men. They also made a concrete promise, which was of more interest to the publicans, that a large supply of spirits would be delivered for free to any publican who was not able to supply their own. It would be delivered so that it could be given away free to all on the last night of legal drinking, to stoke the revolutionary fervour of the ordinary people.

From the size of the party that took place on 29 September, we can assume that the gin showed up even if the revolution didn't. There were a handful of people arrested for shouting 'No Gin, No King' as they paraded thought the streets, but other than that the whole evening passed without much political trouble. In the morning the bodies of drinkers were found slumped asleep in every street and alleyway. When they woke up, it was to a country where gin was illegal. They just ignored the law and kept on drinking.

The perfect drink for the hangover from an all-night binge in mourning of the passing of Madam Geneva was more drink. In addition to gin, publicans offered all kinds of supposed cure-alls and exotic spirits, which were mostly complete fabrications from their own imagination. One of the more popular was usquebaugh, which they claimed was an ancient and authentic Irish recipe. It was nothing of the sort, just a publican's invention; but that didn't stop it being sold as such in inns the length and breadth of England. It has a convincingly medicinal taste, not entirely unlike Jägermeister or Benedictine.

USQUEBAUGH: THE ORIGINAL

To make usquebaugh, or, Irish aqua vitae

Sold there at 18s per quart

*Take two gallons of strong spirits, clear rectified, put them
into an earthen vessel; put thereto a quart of canary sack, two
pounds of raisins well stoned, but not washed; two ounces of
dates well stoned, and the white skins thereof pulled out; two
ounces of cinnamon grossly bruised; four good nutmegs bruised;
an ounce of the best English liquorice, sliced and bruised; six
penny-weights of mace, thirteen penny-weights of the kernels of
apricots, six penny-weights of cloves, twelve penny-weights of
coriander seeds, ten penny-weights of ginger, 1 pound of raisins,
and a pound of dates.*

*Bruise the mace, cloves, kernels, cinnamon and coriander in your
mortar; steep them sixteen days in one quart of strong spirits;
then stew your raisins, and take your liquorice stewed, and
boil the raisins and liquorice in three quarts of water, until it is
reduced to a quart; then draw off your spirits, clean squeezed,
and put one quart more of water in which you have dissolved
three pounds of fine lump sugar.*

*This liquor is commonly used in surfits, being a good stomach
cordial, and is the greatest secret in the trade in Ireland: I only
last December received it from the medical officers there.*

P. Boyle, The Publican and Spirit Dealer's Daily
Companion *(Sixth Edition, c. 1800)*

THE ALCHEMIST'S VERSION

200ml vodka

50ml sweet sherry

1 tsp ground mace

1 tsp whole cloves

1½ tsp whole coriander seeds

1½ tsp ground cinnamon

1 tsp ground ginger

1 tsp apricot kernels (or 2 tsp almonds)

50g raisins

1 x 8cm piece of liquorice root

(or 20g plain liquorice sweets)

20g sugar

Put all the ingredients except the raisins, liquorice and sugar into a large jar with a lid and seal the jar. Leave it to steep for a fortnight, giving it a little shake every couple of days.

After a fortnight, put the raisins, liquorice and sugar into a measuring jug and add boiling water to make up to 100ml. Stir well and leave to cool. Strain the liquorice mixture through a sieve, pressing the excess liquid out gently with a back of a spoon, then add it to the jar with the other ingredients and mix well. Strain the finished mixture through a sieve, and then through a paper coffee filter. Add some green or yellow colouring for an authentic look (this would have been done with saffron or boiled spinach).

Sip your usquebaugh after a meal to settle your stomach, or when you have a hangover from drinking gin all night — or just take a good measure whenever you feel an illness of any kind coming on.

There was some sadness and mourning at the ban, although much of it was just staged to annoy the establishment. Punch houses painted their punchbowls black to put them into mourning, but they didn't give up their trade. An announcement went up that Mother Gin would lie in state at a distiller's shop near St James's Church – a funeral that got the undertaker, his men and all the mourners arrested. But some who had run legal businesses as brandy or rum merchants and could not face the life of a bootlegger were in genuine distress, and there were many reports of suicides.

Londoners were not, at first, left short of a place to get a drink. On the first day of the ban the inmates of the debtors' prisons at the Fleet and King's Bench decided that their situation was already as bad as it could get, and carried on selling drams to anyone who would take them. There were huge queues all day, until the guards gave them a swift reminder of exactly how much worse things could get; they couldn't keep selling gin if they were moved to the windowless cells in the heart of the prison. While the prisoners were stopped from selling gin to outsiders, the guards kept up their normal trade of selling it to their charges without interruption, since they weren't going to turn themselves in and their customers had little chance to turn informer.

Many sellers thought that they could sneak around the law by selling their gin as medicine. Gin was widely used by apothecaries as a cure for all kinds of ailments, and they had been specifically excluded from the first act. Unfortunately that wasn't the case this time around – and even if it had been, a man who was caught at St James's Market was convincing nobody that he was a real apothecary. He was selling gin by the bottle from the back of a cart, having simply tied a large red label to each bottle that read, 'Take two or three spoonfuls of this four or five times a day or as often as the fit takes you'. The label didn't say what exactly the gin could cure; perhaps it was intended for the 'blue devils', the popular term for fits of sadness and despair. The seller was tried, convicted and fined, so he probably could have done with a spoonful or two himself.

Plenty of legitimate apothecaries also found themselves on trial around this time. Many refused on principle to stop selling what they believed was an essential medicine. They were much easier targets for a magistrate who was looking to bring in the lucrative £100 fine for a retailer caught selling gin from a shop, rather than the slippery street vendors who would only be liable for a £10 fine. The apothecaries were also much more likely to be able to pay the fine, even though it would cause them significant hardship; street vendors could be sent for three months imprisonment for failing to pay but there was no profit for the justice in that so only the few who believed in the temperance cause would bother.

Many apothecaries truly did believe that it would be immoral to keep such a potent remedy from the sick who came to them. Others pleaded ignorance, both of the law and of the reason that so many came to their shops for medicinal 'Geneva'. In one trial the prosecutor joked that 'it . . . had been a more sickly time lately than usual', to which the apothecary replied 'that the late Act of Parliament had given many people the gripes'. He didn't get off, but then few did in a justice system that paid judges by the conviction. At least he got a laugh for his money.

People certainly did have plenty of time to spare for jokes at the expense of the establishment. One day a paper appeared on the gate of the palace, when the king was on one of his extended trips to Hanover, saying 'Lost or strayed out of this house, a man who has left a wife and six children on the parish'. The first day after the gin ban, a newspaper also reported a stick-up on Turnham Green. A man was stopped by a single gunman who demanded his money and, when he found that his victim was an MP, informed him that he had become a highwayman because he had been a distiller before the act and 'he was entitled by the Act of Parliament to follow any other calling'.

Legal alternatives to spirits were invented and sold as well. There was cider boiled with pepper to give it a kick, and a mysterious drink called 'tow-row' whose recipe has not survived. Then there was sangree. Invented by an enterprising

Londoner to get around the gin ban, the recipe would be taken over to America and eventually, dropping some letters and evolving a lighter style, settle in Spain as sangria. So if you are ever offered some authentic Spanish sangria, remember that it was really invented one cold September on a small, rainy isle. The original recipe was shrouded in secrecy. It was not only a trade secret, but probably contained a good glug of illegal gin as well. All we know is that it contained 'the finest full-flavour'd Madeira wine'; but I've managed to stitch a good recipe together from later accounts.

SANGREE: THE ALCHEMIST'S VERSION

6 parts good Madeira
1 part lime juice
1 part neat sugar syrup
Nutmeg to taste
1 part gin (optional)

Mix all the ingredients in a small saucepan and warm gently, adding a little grated nutmeg. Serve at blood temperature, with a generous measure of gin added to each glass.

If anyone asks, vehemently deny that you added any gin. No gin here. No gin at all.

One clever plan for getting around the ban was published in the form of a conversation in several newspapers. It was a nice idea, but was shot down as a defence the first time it came up in court. It went something like this:

'My dear publican, I would like to buy two gallons of gin. But alas, I don't have all of the money on my person.'

'That's all right, sir; I can sell it to you on credit, and you can pay a little at a time.'

'But there is another problem: I have a shortage of storage space. May I take it away a little at a time as well?'

'Certainly, sir. Why don't you pay the first penny, and I will give you the first dram?'

While some occupied themselves with clever schemes and a few poor apothecaries ended up in the dock, most people were carrying on almost as normal, since without enough money to pay the fine they had little to fear. There was no police force, and it was in the interests of the excise men and judges enforcing the law to convict only those who could pay, since the sole income from the role was their share of any fines that were paid. On every corner there was still a barrow selling gin, or a market woman with a bottle hidden up her skirts, protected by their own poverty.

With illegal gin sold from under a stranger's skirt, you couldn't be sure what you were getting. Gins had fancy names like White Satin, Blue Ruin, Cuckold's Delight, King Theodore of Corsica, Flashes of Lightning or The

Cure for the Blue Devils, but they were usually more turpentine than juniper. Even the less dodgy recipes for gin – those involving real juniper – were full of toxic ingredients. They were used in all kinds of food and drink at the time because their toxic properties just weren't known. It wouldn't be safe to try a truly authentic recipe for bootleg gin, but I have managed to put together a cocktail that should give you some idea of the taste without any of the nasty side effects.

BOOTLEG GIN: THE ORIGINAL

For twenty gallons of gin

Seventeen gallons of spirits one to five under proof. Take one penny-weight and three quarters of the oil of vitriol, one penny-weight and three quarters of the oil of almonds, half a penny-weight of the oil of turpentine, two penny-weights of the oil of juniper berries, mixed with lump sugar and spirits of wine, as before; add to it one pint of lime-water, and one pint of rose-water; use the whole. After you dissolve five pounds of lump sugar, in two gallons and a half of water that was boiled, as before directed, fine it down with the proportioned quantity of allum and salt of tartar.

P. *Boyle*, The Publican and Spirit Dealer's Daily Companion (*Sixth Edition, c. 1800*)

88

THE ALCHEMIST'S VERSION

1 part vodka

½ part retsina

¼ part amaretto

¼ part neat sugar syrup

⅛ part rosewater

½ part water

1–2 drops of juniper oil

Simply mix and serve. But how? With tonic? While this gin would be really lovely with tonic, that wouldn't be authentic. Tonic wouldn't be introduced to Britain for more than another hundred years; so while you could drink it with tonic, it would be a little like going to a re-enactment wearing a digital watch. Chilled or with ice? Although this gin would also be excellent shaken over ice with a splash of vermouth and served in a well-chilled Martini glass, historical authenticity will not allow.

Drink it the authentic way. Just add a little water and drink at room/street temperature. If possible, try to throw some mud at an MP, or anyone who looks like they might be rich or important, at the same time. That's the eighteenth-century way!

There was one place where you might get a better quality of gin – the only kind of gin shop that could stay in one place without too much fear of informers for long enough to develop a reputation for good gin: the Puss and Mew shop. There's a wonderfully colourful tale in the biography *The Life and Uncommon Adventures of Captain Dudley Bradstreet* about how the shop was invented. Bradstreet was quite a character, and his biography is full of unlikely anecdotes. It's about as likely that he actually invented the Puss and Mew shop in anything like the way that he describes as it is that he really turned back Bonnie Prince Charlie's army single-handed. But since he tells such a good story, it's much more fun to believe him than to call him a liar.

In 1736, after a spell as a government spy, Irish adventurer Captain Bradstreet arrived in London on the promise of an army commission. When the commission failed to appear, he was left in a strange city with only a few pounds to his name – but he was a resourceful man, and an educated one. He took a copy of the Gin Act and read it through. He found that for an informer to turn him in they had to know his name, and he also found that it was illegal, even for a magistrate, to break down his doors to find it out.

He had a friend rent a small house and lend him the keys so that not even the landlord would know his name. Then he bought a large picture of a cat. Why a cat? We will probably never know. Perhaps it just happened to be the first picture he found that was the right size for the window. He got his cat, and he nailed it up so that it covered his window. Then he cut a hole for its mouth and pushed a small pipe out under its paw, which he bent up to a funnel inside the house. He told a few local gossips that his magic cat would give gin to anyone who fed it pennies, and he shut himself up for business.

The first day was slow, alone with his magic cat; but soon he had so many visitors coming to feed that cat and call, 'Puss, Puss, give me two pennyworth of gin' that his neighbours had trouble getting in and out of their houses. It was at that point he decided that he was lonely, and invited a beautiful prostitute to assist him. The rest of his story is far too lurid for these pages, but he did keep up the business in good company for a few months – until imitators started cutting into his trade. Then he moved onto new and even more improbable schemes. As a result, all over town you could find the sign of the cat and call out 'Puss!' to be answered with a 'Mew!' and a glass of gin passed through a hole, poured through a pipe or delivered to you via a drawer. The magic cat had multiplied!

The Puss and Mew houses were set up to evade a new threat: the informers. To begin with they were just opportunists: hand someone in who could afford to pay their fine, and you got to keep half. Five pounds was a lot of money, and many were desperate enough to risk the anger of their neighbours. The neighbours were indeed furious when it happened, and they did what they had always done to shame someone who had broken their social code: traditional punishments known as 'rough music'.

On 17 January 1737, an informer called Pullin got a nasty surprise. There was a mob outside his home carrying an effigy of him. They carried it all around the streets of the St George parish to Hanover Square, where they tied it to a pole, built a pile of wood beneath it and burned it. Another informer was made to ride backwards on an ass and paraded up and down Bond Street while the crowd jeered him and pelted him with mud. There were many incidents like this one, but initially, none were violent. The informers were embarrassed and probably scared, but they were in no real danger.

That changed later in the year. Prohibition wasn't working, but the government was so afraid of the people and of a Jacobite rebellion that it was unwilling to compromise. It wanted to prove that it could enforce the law as it stood, and it was willing to pay for it. The new enforcement measures passed through Parliament hidden in a law called the Sweets Act – a bill to encourage the production of fruit wines, which some foolishly thought could replace gin in the nation's heart. The bill promised that the five-pound reward would be paid to any informer who got a conviction, whether the fine was paid or not. Anyone convicted who could not pay the fine was sent for three months in Bridewell prison, as they would have been before had anyone bothered to convict them; only now they were also whipped bloody when they were released.

Fruit wines like those encouraged by the Act were a traditional part of the publican's stock, even if they were old-fashioned and unpopular by this time. There are plenty of recipes if you'd like to get a taste of the failed gin alternative, and I've picked a nice easy one. We're still in proper brewing territory here, though, so you will need a few special pieces of equipment; but you can get a plastic demijohn, brewer's yeast, steriliser and a bubble lock from a homebrew shop for less than a fiver.

APRICOT WINE: THE ORIGINAL

Put three pounds of sugar into three quarts of water, let them boil together, and scum it well; then put in six pounds of apricots pared and stoned and let them boil till they are tender; take out the apricots, and when the liquor is cold, bottle it for the present use. The apricots will make good marmalade. You may use one pint of clear spirits to every gallon.

P. *Boyle*, The Publican and Spirit Dealer's Daily Companion (*Sixth Edition, c. 1800*)

THE ALCHEMIST'S VERSION

Ingredients:
3kg apricots, halved and stoned
1.5kg sugar
1 packet brewer's yeast (champagne yeast is
best, but any wine yeast will do)

Equipment:
Large soup pan (if you're not sure your pan is large
enough, you can split the fruit into two batches)

Large funnel
5-litre demijohn
Cheesecloth or jelly bag
Bubble lock

Put the apricots and sugar in the pan and cover with 2 litres of water. Boil until the apricots are tender, then set aside to cool. While the apricots are cooling, activate your yeast by following the instructions on the packet. Once the apricots are cool, put the funnel in the mouth of the demijohn and stretch the cheesecloth or jelly bag over the funnel (you'll want someone else to hold this steady). Strain the liquid through the cloth, tipping the fruit in last. Gather the cloth into a bag around the remaining fruit and give it a good squeeze. Add the yeast to the demijohn, give it a swirl, seal with your bubble lock and leave in a warm place until the bubbles stop (2–3 weeks). Siphon the wine off into bottles, leaving the sediment behind. You have made your very own fruit wine!

Swig your wine from a clay tankard with a good measure of spirits added in, if you find your drink needs an extra kick and you are sure there are no informers about.

With so much money at stake after the Sweets Act had passed, the informers started to turn professional and organised, and the mob began to turn violent in reaction to this perceived persecution. The first serious attack was less than a month after the new law was passed. Informers were pelted with mud, sticks and stones. They were ducked in the Thames and dragged through the streets to be 'pumped' by sticking their head under the running water at every water pump in the district. The first death was in July; four more followed, including one woman. The informers weren't even allowed to go quietly to their graves. Their funerals would be disrupted by people pelting the coffin and mourners with mud, while others played improvised instruments to make a huge musical din.

The informers prospered as long as they were encouraged and believed by the courts. One particular judge presided over more gin trials than any other, and was also the most hated by the populace: Thomas De Veil. He was a 'working justice', a man with a noble name but little money who lived on the fines he imposed in his court. It was at his house that the first real riot happened – the one that had been predicted, but had not materialised, on the first day of the ban.

The day before the riot, a man called Edward Arnold had followed some informers home and caused a disturbance outside their house, threatening to tear it down and kill them. He was arrested, and De Veil sent him to Newgate. As soon as word got round that Arnold had been jailed just for calling out the informers, a mob formed around the judge's house. Soon there were nearly a thousand people swarming the narrow street, climbing up the shop signs and baying for blood. De Veil read the Riot Act, but it had no effect, and it took the arrival of soldiers to break up the mob.

The next day one Roger Allen, who had been iden-tified as a ringleader, was arrested and sent to Newgate under the Riot Act to await trial. The results of the trial were to be a fantastic surprise to a confident establish-ment. They didn't think that the trial could possibly go wrong. Allen was obviously guilty. He had been there at the head of a thousand-person mob, threatening a mag-istrate. The mob had seen him, the magistrate and the two informers had seen him from the window, and it had been reported in all the papers that he had been there. There was no way that he could possibly deny it. On the day of the trial, the hall and surrounding streets were so crowded that it was said you could have walked a quarter mile across people's heads.

The first move by Roger Allen's lawyer was to insist that the jury could not contain anyone of rank. This was to be a true jury of his peers – trial of the poor, by the poor. Once his defence had a jury that they liked, they chose a strategy that no one would have expected: they declared their client insane. There was no way to deny what he had done, and because of that, the jury couldn't do anything except convict him, even though they really did not want to. They needed a plausible excuse to let him go, and now the lawyer had given them one. After some persuasive testimony from his mother and his master, the verdict was unanimous. Roger

Allen was free – and legally insane. Outside the court, he declared to the crowd that: 'The great liberty of mobbing a justice now and then, and my own life, had certainly been lost, if I had not had wit enough to prove myself a fool.'

From then on, the mob was merciless. It only took one cry of 'Informers!' to bring dozens of people to your aid, improvised weapons at the ready. Many who were convicted and sent to Bridewell were then rescued by the mob as officers were taking them from the court to the prison. Others helped to save themselves and others from the informers in their own creative ways. One Bristol informer was given a bottle of vinegar in place of gin by a suspicious gin-seller. He took it straight to the justices without trying it, and found himself charged with contempt of court and put in the stocks when they tested it. It was easy for the mob to find him in the stocks and, informed of what he'd done, they gave him their own brand of punishment for his trouble: he was tarred and feathered.

It wasn't enough to check the gin when you bought it, either. One young lad, probably a first-time informer, was foolish enough to stop off on his way to the court and boast to his friends about what he was going to do. They distracted him just long enough to drink all of the gin and replace it with their own piss. He took it to none other than Thomas De Veil, who poured himself a glass and tasted it. This sent him into a furious rage, and the boy was sent straight to Newgate for contempt.

By now, the only people who dared to inform were

professionals, who were as likely to make the charges up as to bring real ones, even though there was no shortage of real gin-sellers. Many of the justices themselves, unlike De Veil, grew to dislike and distrust the informers, and would rule against them where they could. John Lade had two informers come before him with a bowl of punch from a local pub. Presented with the physical evidence, he was unable to deny the allegation, so he did his duty, convicted the publican and fined him ten pounds. Once he had paid his fine, the publican accused the two informers of having stolen his bowl. With the bowl in his hands, the judge immediately agreed, and sent both informers to the county jail for theft.

The justice system was fighting with itself. Justice Clifford William Phillips was charged with obstructing justice when he turned up at another judge's court while it was in session. He knew the woman who was on trial, and he told Justice Thomas Farmer exactly what he thought of the 'rascally scoundrell fellows of informers' who were giving evidence. He proclaimed to the court that Farmer was committing a great injustice by encouraging them at the expense of the hard-working poor, and that by it he would earn the curse of all poor persons. He was disciplined, but he was not convicted, and the local overseers of the poor wrote to the Lord High Chancellor on his behalf to tell him that Phillips had 'acquired the love and esteem of all . . . our parish by his knowledge and impartiality in the discharge of his duty'.

Even the churchwardens, who received half of the fines for the relief of the poor, did not want to be part of the system of informers and punishments. The fines were a source of income for their charity work, but many of those who sold gin were the poorest of their parishes. Deprived of the occupation of selling gin, they would have no other means of support, increasing the numbers in need of poor relief far beyond the income from the fines. Those who looked after the poor every day could see that depriving so many people of their livelihoods was a greater evil than the possibility of some drinking gin to excess. Most of the parishes began simply returning the half of the fine they were given to the person who paid it. After all, they were given the money to distribute to the poor – and after losing ten pounds, the convicted gin-sellers were very poor.

Gin-sellers and their customers were typically not just poor, but also cold. In the days before central heating, keeping warm could be difficult, and so it was common to drink just about anything that could be heated hot. One of the favourite drinks was called 'gin & hot', a hot mixture of ale and gin. I've tried it out on a few willing victims and received a mixture of confused enjoyment and absolute disgust; I guess it must be an acquired taste. Usually the drinks were heated up by plunging a red-hot poker into the cup, which was easy and wonderfully dramatic, but did have a tendency to get ash in your drink.

GIN & HOT: THE ALCHEMIST'S VERSION

Ingredients:
25ml gin
25ml sugar syrup
½ pint ale

Equipment:
Sharpening steel (or other suitable clean metal utensil;
just be sure it doesn't have a plastic handle)
Oven glove
Large mug (or suitably heat-resistant glass; an
old-fashioned dimple glass with a handle is perfect)

Put the sharpening steel into a hot oven for 10–15 minutes until thoroughly heated. Put the gin and syrup into your mug, and then top up with the ale. Carefully take your hot steel out of the oven using an oven glove, making sure you have a good grip. Plunge your steel into the mug and stir.

Enjoy the dramatic sizzle as the iron plunges in and then sip your warm, foamy mug of gin & hot.

The tricks used by informers ranged from the unusual to the downright nasty. One of the most common and most hated tactics was to feign sickness or to beg for some medicinal gin for a sick relative, sick friend or even a sick horse.

One informer was so dedicated to her sham illness that she went to a barber-surgeon and asked to be bled. Only when she had given a bowl or two of blood did she pretend to faint and ask for the reviving dram. The surgeon gave it to her, unable to believe that a lady would go so far as to give up her blood to catch him. He soon learned that he was mistaken.

Informers started to form gangs so that they could gather information and inform outside of their own boroughs, where they were too likely to be recognised. However, it was difficult for Londoners to find trusted associates outside their own areas. People, especially the poor, did not in general travel and mingle between boroughs. Luckily there was no shortage of crooked excise men willing to aid in the introductions.

The scale and organisation of the informer network would truly come to light with the downfall of one man, Edward Parker. He was just a lowly excise officer, working to ensure duty was paid on candles, when the new gin division found itself in need of officers. He wasn't slow to volunteer – he knew there was money to be made in the new division – but his first attempts certainly didn't look like the work of a criminal mastermind. Parker went with another officer to the county jail to try for a dram, and they did manage to get one; but the officers needed to know the seller's name before they could convict him. As soon as they started asking too many questions, the inmates got suspicious. They beat both the officers to within an inch of their lives. They survived – but three months later, clever Parker was back in the hospital again after another beating.

Two beatings must have been the number needed to knock some sense into him, because it was then that he realised he could get others to do his dirty work. Maybe they would be better at it than he was, but even if not, at least it wasn't his skin at risk. He soon developed a network of informers who he paid to give information: a guinea if the gin-seller paid the fine, and half a guinea if they went to Bridewell. It didn't matter to Parker whether they were guilty or not, provided the informer could get them fined. When a new member was initiated into Parker's network, they were encouraged to start by giving information against anyone they disliked, resented or owed money to. Sometimes informers would work together in groups and come to court together; at other times, one would act as informer while another played the role of a stranger who just happened to see and felt obliged to come forward. Some judges might be suspicious of their characters, and of the familiar faces that kept turning up, but most were too busy enforcing the new law and taking the fines to pay much attention to who their informers were.

It got even easier for Edward Parker in April 1738, when he was appointed to a new role in the special sessions of the court: testifying to the character of the witnesses. It was a dream job for him, and over the next eight months more than 300 people passed through that court. Most were convicted, thanks to his pet informers, netting him up to four pounds each. He even tried to have a magistrate – the same Justice Phillips who had disrupted a trial, and who strongly opposed the use of informers – convicted for encouraging people to break the Gin Act, and for questioning the character of one of Parker's informers. He was overreaching himself when he tried to get to a judge, and he failed. No matter how bad things got, no one was about to allow a lowly excise man to have a judge convicted – but the attempt showed just how high Parker's opinion of himself had become.

That was the beginning of his decline. The courts were starting to run out of money. Paying five pounds to an informer for every soul sent to Bridewell was an expensive business. Informers were starting to come away with nothing more than IOUs, unless they were Parker's informers. He had to take the IOU but keep paying them their guinea, running down the reserves of money he had already made while he got nothing but IOUs. His luck was running out, too. He had been too careless and too greedy. Rumours had started circulating, at first just in Westminster, but soon also in the popular press. On 4 December 1738, he didn't show up for work. The next week, indictments were filed against him for perjury and embezzlement. Not content with taking the informers' bounty, it seemed he had also been embezzling the half of the fine intended for poor relief.

Parker died soon afterwards, before his own case could come up before the magistrates. The papers didn't clearly state the cause of his death, but it doesn't seem unlikely that he took his own life. He left barely enough cash to pay for his own funeral, but his executors put in a claim at the excise office for £1,535 due for information given. That was only the money he had a legitimate claim to, and even that much was a fortune at the time. It was believed that he had played a part in the convictions of over 1,500 people in a little over a year. His funeral was held in secret to prevent the angry mob from tearing his corpse to pieces – a sensible precaution. When the body of a female informer was buried in St Giles after her suicide, she was disinterred by her neighbours, who, perhaps confusing her momentarily with a vampire, drove a stake through her heart.

Amid much moralising by the same press who had demanded the gin laws that created him, the last word on Parker came from the *London Evening Post*: 'Tis said he died in miserable conditions as such rascals generally do.'

Plenty of gin toasts were drunk at his passing, and given the special occasion, some may even have raised a glass of celebratory punch. Punch began mainly as a drink for the rich, made with expensive tea and brandy, but soon cheaper versions began springing up, made with gin and fruit juices. For a celebration, though – like the death of a notorious informer baron – you really have to go back to the finer things.

PUNCH FOR A CELEBRATION: THE ALCHEMIST'S VERSION

2½ parts cold Earl Grey tea

2 parts best brandy

1 part orange juice

1 part sugar syrup

½ part lime juice

Simply mix and serve at room temperature in a ceramic
punchbowl, with a ladle and fine cups. If you can have
'RIP Edward Parker' glazed on the inside, all the better.

Although it would be four more years before the Gin Act was officially repealed, with the money running out the will to enforce it had all but gone. Even the only two people in the whole country to actually take out the £50 licence wrote to the excise office officially returning their licences. Both had been brought to court and convicted, despite the licence, on a technicality. They told the commission that they were surrendering their licences because they were 'accompanied with great incumberances and ill conveniences as not to be surmounted'.

Besides, war had broken out with Spain, leaving the government occupied with more important matters and giving the mob an efficient method of ridding society of the few remaining informers. After begrudgingly paying their fine, the victim could then follow the informers until they met up with the rest of their gang. Once you'd located them, it was only a matter of finding the nearest press gang and telling them where they could find a group of young men just perfect for the navy. Every five pounds an informer made came with the risk of buying themselves a one-way ticket on a warship bound for Spain.

The press gangs wouldn't turn down the offer of a few good men. They would try any scheme to hunt out likely (or unlikely) recruits. This one, as reported in *The Monthly Chronologer*, published in August 1738, had nothing to do with gin but demonstrates the lengths to which they were willing to go, and is just such a good story that I found it impossible to resist including it: 'On Saturday last some sailors went up the Monument and placed a live turkey on the top thereof, which in a short time drew a prodigious number of gazers, by which means the press-gangs in the street pick'd up a great number of proper persons for manning his majesty's fleet.'

The press gangs were already keen, but publicans were so happy to get rid of their informers that often they would even offer an extra reward. One publican was so pleased to have the informer who had brought him to court removed that he bought barrels of ale for the whole crew of the ship that took him away.

In 1743 the law was finally repealed and replaced instead by some more modest and enforceable measures to raise money for the war chest. A duty of sixpence a gallon on spirits at the point of production, and a £1 retail licence, would bring gin back out of the shadows and make her profitable. Having a war to deal with, Parliament lost all interest in gin, except for its potential to earn them some cash. It worked like a charm, making them £20,000 from licences and £90,000 from duty in the first year alone. Madam Geneva was legal and welcome once again. She was back on the streets that she had never truly left.

Prohibition was remembered in Thomas De Veil's official biography as the 'boldest experiment . . . ever made in a free country', but most remembered the story more as it was told by these two earls, speaking in the House of Lords debate on the repeal of the Gin Act:

If the promoter of the bill against gin had not been known to be a very sober man, I should have supposed him to be an excessive gin-drinker.

– Earl of Chesterfield

The law . . . was passed in a sort of mad fit, and has been an affront to our government ever since it passed. Every man that could foresee any thing, forsaw, that it was such a law as could never be executed. But as the poor had run gin-mad, the rich had run anti-gin-mad and in this fit of madness no one would give ear to reason.

– Earl of Ilay

CHAPTER FOUR

PURE IRISH SPIRIT

I know that I'll get into trouble for including a chapter about Ireland in a book calling itself a British history, but this book is really the history of people defying the British authorities. The Irish have always been the very best at doing that. To leave them out would mean missing one of the most spirited periods of excise defiance; so hopefully I will be forgiven my impertinence.

When the taxman first came for poitín, making it was not only a long-standing tradition in Ireland but was also the only way that many tenant farmers could afford to pay their rents. Poor roads and remote locations made it difficult to transport bulky grain to market, whereas moving poitín was much simpler. Some farmers even paid their rents directly in poitín rather than money.

Poitín as we now know it – or at least, the stuff that tourists are allowed to get hold of – is usually distilled from sugar, treacle, potatoes or whatever else is currently cheap and easily available, often without too much regard for taste. Originally, however, malted barley would have been used, and the poitín makers would have produced a whiskey nearly indistinguishable from an unaged Scottish single malt, apart from the insistence on including an 'e' in the name. The name poitín means 'little pot', in reference to the small pot stills in which it was made, which would also have been similar to the copper stills in use in Scotland. The poitín was slow-distilled, and for many years it was hugely superior to the rushed, raw corn product of the few licensed stills in the country. It was only in later years, as the poitín producers became more endangered and as sugar became both cheaper and more easily available than malt, that the nature of poitín began to change to make it a distinct product from whiskey.

But what would a treacle poitín taste like? It's closest in taste to rum, since both are made with sugar cane; but whereas rum is generally made from the light molasses produced at the beginning of the sugar refining process, the kind of black treacle that would be used for poitín is produced at the very end of the process. Treacle has a lot of extra dark, acidic flavours, and distilling the treacle mixture leaves the spirit clear but still with some of those sharp, heavy flavours that make it taste somewhat different to rum. Without a still to hand you'll have to put up with the colour, but you can make something that tastes similar.

TREACLE POITÍN: THE ALCHEMIST'S VERSION

4 tbsp black treacle

4 tbsp water

200ml white rum (overproof if you can get it)

Put the treacle and water into a small saucepan and heat gently until the treacle has completely dissolved. Allow to cool to room temperature, seal in a small container and leave in the freezer overnight. Pass the treacle mixture through a paper coffee filter while still cold, then add to the rum and mix well.

Drink while swearing to anyone who asks that you made it yourself to your grandaddy's recipe.

When excise duty was first introduced to Ireland in 1644 the island was treated, not as a part of Britain, but as the nearest colony – which meant that it was treated very badly. Trade laws were restrictive, and most of the land was divided up into estates owned by British gentry who had never set foot there but who still wanted to extract as much money from their estates as possible. They leased large parcels of land, two or three compete townships, to middlemen on long leases, who would then let smaller sections to farmers on a short-term basis, extracting both the large rents required by the absent gentry and a sizeable profit for themselves.

Because the middlemen's leases were long, but not permanent, they had little motivation to invest for the long term by improving land or industry to provide an alternative income to poitín-making. They also had little motivation to assist in excise collection or in the prevention of illicit distilling. The excise was collected in a similarly hands-off way by contracting the collection out to 'excise farmers', who paid the crown a set amount they had bid for the role and then collected what they could. This mostly meant coming to agreements with large distillers and leaving the small ones alone, as they weren't worth trying to chase. With no one motivated to do anything about it, for a while poitín-making could go on uninterrupted.

The excise ended farming in 1682 and began relying on salaried officers, a change that could have put the poitín makers in danger if serious enforcers had been appointed. Instead, since excise officer positions were profitable ones to hold, they ended up being distributed as political favours or though family connections, and in some cases the positions were even hereditary. They went to gentry or other people of influence and were often treated as a reward, not as a job requiring hard work. There was little danger of these pampered men, out for profit, becoming serious enforcers. The excise men instead became a byword for incompetence and corruption. This was never clearer that when Arthur Terry, the collector at the port of Derry, was taken to court by the excise service for fraud. His own defence, to which he swore under oath, was that both he and his deputy (who was also his son) were not intentionally committing fraud, but were simply incompetent and had no idea how to even keep accounts. The court believed him.

Corruption wasn't limited to ignoring unlicensed distillers; most officers also accepted bribes from the licensed distillers to report and tax only a portion of the spirit distilled. This problem was endemic despite some half-hearted efforts by the excise to prevent at least the most obvious abuses. One gauger, James McKee, was dismissed from his post when it was discovered that he was not only accepting bribes but also giving receipts for them. In mitigation, he pleaded that he was drunk when he accepted the bribes, and unbelievably, this was taken into account. In another case, John White, near Rathmullen, managed to get a post as a revenue assistant even though he was already a licensed distiller himself. He made a most thorough check of his own operation, I'm sure, but he was drummed out of town by the local illicit distillers before the excise even had a chance to dismiss him for fraud.

Rather than try hiring more competent, less corrupt officers, the authorities tried to improve the rate of collection by giving the existing gaugers more powers, making collecting the excise duty both easier and more profitable for them. This eventually resulted in a 1731 law that restricted distilling entirely to market towns, making it illegal to distil in the countryside at all. Since profit seemed to be the only motivation that the gaugers understood, there were also bounties introduced for any unlicensed stills that they captured and surrendered. Properly motivated, they began to get out into the countryside and hunt for stills. As soon as they started still-hunting, the job went from a sedate and peaceful one, only annoying the licensed distillers, to one that was widely reviled and carried a real danger of violence and even of death.

For those in the towns who tried to work within the law and remain as licensed distillers, the situation got progressively worse. Distillation was further restricted from any market town to only the largest towns, and minimum still sizes were introduced so that licensed distillers had to use a still holding at least 200 gallons. The final nail in the coffin of any remaining small distillers came in 1881, when the legal minimum quantity was introduced, and it was increased with every passing year.

Most legal distillers distilled only as needed, perhaps only as often as once a month, but by 1887 the legal minimum quantity meant that they would be charged duty on five distillations a week whether they performed them or not. Five distillations a week on the minimum 200-gallon still would produce far more than the market in most towns could possibly absorb, and most distillers either shut down or went dark, moving their operation and becoming illicit distillers. In County Donegal the number of legal distillers dropped from thirty-nine to none, in Strabane from seventy-four to none, in Armagh from seventy-four to nine; and the situation was similar in other counties the length and breadth of the country.

The few legal distilleries that did remain were in the largest towns, mostly in Dublin, and in order to keep up with the required schedule they gave up the use of malt and started producing raw grain spirit, hastily distilled. The government's theory was that with distilling now restricted to a few large operations, the Revenue would be able to keep a close eye on them. The politician's ideas proved as divorced from reality as ever. In practice, bribes just continued on a larger scale as the distilleries they could be extracted from also grew larger and fewer. If they were kept properly lubricated, the excise officers would arrive at the exact same time every day, to allow any whiskey that had been produced but not accounted for to be kept well out of their way. They would even sometimes make their entries in the distiller's books in erasable ink so that the distillers could edit them later at their leisure. Meanwhile, in all the areas that were left without any legal distillers, poitín was there to fill the void. Even in areas that did have a licensed distiller, poitín was both cheaper and better than the legal 'Parliament whiskey'.

Although we have now developed the habit of throwing whiskey into any hot drink or dessert and calling it Irish, it would traditionally have been rare to drink poitín in any way other than straight. After so much risk and hard work to get the alcohol so strong, it would have been a terrible waste to cook any of that strength out again. Even if you can't put whiskey into your dessert while remaining historically accurate, you can cook up a good authentic dessert to accompany it, like an oatmeal flummery. The recipe I have used here is from an English cookbook. The dish was common throughout England, Scotland and Wales, but it was also common enough in Ireland that it crops up on the menus of institutions such as prisons as a suitable substitute for milk when none is to be had.

OATMEAL FLUMMERY: THE ORIGINAL

Get some oatmeal, put it into a broad deep pan, then cover it with water, stir it together, and let it stand twelve hours, then pour off that water clear, and put in a good deal of fresh water, stir it again in twelve hours, and soon in twelve more, then pour off the water clear, and strain the oatmeal through a coarse hair-sieve, and pour it into a saucepan, keeping it stirring all the time with a stick till it boils and is very thick; then pour it into dishes; when cold turn it into plates, and eat it with what you please, either wine and sugar, or beer with sugar, or milk. It eats very pretty with cyder and sugar.

Hannah Glasse, The Art of Cookery Made Plain and Easy *(1747)*

THE ALCHEMIST'S VERSION

200g oatmeal
Plenty of water
Even more patience

Put the oatmeal into a glass or ceramic bowl and cover with 600ml of cold water. Stir and leave to sit for at least 12 hours. Once every 12 hours, without disturbing the oatmeal that has settled to the bottom, pour the water off the top until you reach a point where you risk losing oatmeal. Top the bowl back up to the previous level, stir and leave for another 12 hours. Repeat the process until the oatmeal has been soaking for at least 48 hours in total.

After 48 hours (or longer if you want your pudding a little more tangy), pour off the top layer of water again, then tip the wet oatmeal mixture into a sieve resting over a clean saucepan. Press as much liquid out of the oatmeal with the back of a spoon as you can, and then set it aside. It's the water we're going to use to make the flummery, but you can still use the oatmeal to make porridge if you like. Waste not, want not.

Bring the oat liquid to the boil and then let it simmer, stirring constantly, until it begins to thicken. Be prepared for this to take some time, as much as 20 minutes or half an hour. Once it starts to thicken, keep a close eye on it and keep it simmering until it gets very thick, like custard. Pour the mixture into small pots or onto shallow dishes, and put in the fridge to set.

Serve with milk and sugar on top, if you have such luxuries available, and a good glass of whiskey or poitín to wash it down.

As one of their new powers, the excise officers now had the right to have the military accompany them on their outings to seize stills. In return, the military officers were supposed to get a share of the bounty when the seizure was successful, and when the gaugers routinely tried to cheat them out of their share of the bounty they became highly uncooperative. While they couldn't refuse to go on the still-hunting expeditions altogether, they would approach the distilling sites as loudly and slowly as possible, shouting orders and shouldering arms, to give the distillers time to escape. The grateful distillers would leave a few jugs of poitín behind for the military to find, a much more certain reward than the bounty from the gauger.

While the military did have to accompany the gaugers when requested, they were not required to assist in the actual seizure. This resulted in one incident where two gaugers were trying to break down the door of a house to seize a still while the military watched from a short distance away. From where they were standing, the soldiers could see the occupants taking everything out through the back door and away over the hill behind the house. They didn't even mention it to the excise officers. By the time the door was broken down the house was, of course, completely empty of any evidence of distilling.

Although their military escorts were troublesome, the gaugers were still best not to go without them, since the dangers that they faced were real. One excise officer, Aeneas Coffrey, was making a seizure in Carthage when he wandered a little too far from his military escort. He was set upon by fifty men, and only survived until his escort was able to come and rescue him because his attackers were so keen to hurt him that they kept getting in each other's way. He received a fractured skull, two bayonet wounds and a host of other cuts and bruises. It took weeks for him to recover from the attack.

Excise officers weren't even safe in the courtrooms. Five years later, the same officer nearly had his skull fractured again when a large rock grazed his head while he was giving evidence at a trial. Other excise officers never even made it to the stand. In 1815, around Donegal and Tyrone, there were a number of kidnappings of excise officers, intended to prevent them giving evidence and generally succeeding. The gaugers were tossed into sacks and held somewhere out of the way until the court session was finished. Most would just be in a nearby house or barn, but some were less lucky. One officer was kidnapped, nearly drowned and taken away to an island in Lough Veagh, where he was kept continuously drunk and forced to work the still for six weeks before he was finally released. A kidnap attempt in Letterkenny was foiled only because the kidnappers were kicked by their own horse as they tried to get William Hendrick tied securely to its saddle. The horse caused just enough delay that a nearby army detachment began to approach. At that point the kidnappers decided that they had better just give up the attempt and flee.

The violence was not all one way; many gaugers were just as violent towards the local population. Once the job became less cushy and more risky, it began to attract some dangerous characters. James Nugent was a particularly unpleasant man who had been transferred from Fermanagh to Killybegs after he offended the local gentry so much that he could not stay. On his arrival he began a long-standing feud with one of the legal distillers in the area, John Armstrong. After several years of violence and accusations on both sides, things came to an unpleasant end when Nugent had Armstrong's son transported to Australia as a vagabond.

Matters came to a head in Donegal in 1783, when a party of gaugers and soldiers were transporting a still found near Killygordon. A mob attempted to retrieve the still, and the gaugers gave the order to open fire, killing four and wounding six. A coroner returned a verdict of wilful murder, but the soldiers and the gaugers all fled the county before charges could be brought. Unfortunately this would be just the first in a series of incidents of casual violence by excise officers and by the few army units who could be persuaded to cooperate with them.

Three years later, in Ballyshannon, the army were coming into the town on market day to search for stills when a large crowd prevented them from crossing the bridge from their barracks into the town. They returned to their barracks and began to fire indiscriminately out of the windows at anyone seen on the bridge, without warning. Once the bridge cleared they began to run up the street, firing at random through doors and windows. Twenty-two were wounded and two killed, both young women. One of the injured was a five-year-old boy who was shot in the arm while he was inside his grandfather's house.

The outcry after the massacre was huge, with even the local magistrate getting involved and demanding answers. In the aftermath of the incident it was revealed that the soldiers had been drunk and that their commanders had left to have dinner, leaving only an ensign in charge. The Major in charge of the unit refused to name the soldiers involved, had them moved out of the county when their names were finally revealed and, when he could not avoid giving them up to the court any longer, influenced the judge and undermined the credibility of the witnesses. His attempts to obstruct justice were so successful that all of the soldiers were acquitted except for one private, who was found guilty of the murder of Elinor Madden even though it was generally believed that he was not the one who had fired the shot.

In reaction to the use of guns against unarmed civilians, the smugglers began to get armed themselves. The crew of a Revenue cutter discovered this new development for themselves when they tried to come ashore at Moville. They were ambushed the moment they set foot on the shore. Every single member of the crew was shot and injured, although none were killed and they were eventually able to get away.

The attacks on the most hated of the revenue officers were relentless. In Carndonagh, a gauger was shot with a pistol while he was making his rounds. A few days later, when he went for a short walk with his wife to aid in his recovery from the first gunshot wound, he was shot again by a man on a horse. The Revenue offered a £100 reward for information leading to the capture of the culprit – such a huge sum that it led to five men being incarcerated for the attempted murder, even though at most two men could have committed the crime.

In 1767 there was a brief lull in distilling and the revenue service congratulated themselves on their success; but the lull was actually just the result of a poor grain harvest that year, and nothing to do with their efforts. Despite the shortage, in many places people would still produce poitín from the little grain that they had, leaving none to eat. The rent still had to be paid, the absentee landlords didn't know or care that there was a famine, and poitín was still the best cash crop available, even if it did consume much-needed food. Once the grain was gone the farmers and their families instead had to eat whatever foraged food they could find: herbs, nuts and berries. Some berries weren't edible on their own because they were so bitter, but they could be brought back anyway and added to the poitín to flavour it and possibly give it a little extra nutritional value. The berries were sloes, which are now highly sought after in England for use in gin, but they originate from Ireland and make an amazing whiskey liqueur.

SLOE POITÍN: THE ALCHEMIST'S VERSION

*A punnet of sloes (it's great to pick your own, but
you can also buy them online if you can't)
One full bottle of poitín and another empty one (you
can find some legally produced poitíns in the shops
these days, but you can also use whiskey instead)*

For authenticity, you should prick all of the berries individually
with a thorn of the bush from which you picked them. If you
haven't got the patience for that, you can pop them in the freezer
overnight instead and then thaw them thoroughly. Half-fill the
empty bottle with pricked or defrosted sloes, then top it up with
poitín until it's full and seal. Leave your sloe poitín in a cool,
dark place for at least three months. Then it's ready to drink! You
can strain the sloes out if you want to be neat, but you can also
just pour it a measure at a time while leaving them in.

Traditionally, sloe poitín would not have been sweetened, since
there would have been little sugar available to sweeten it with;
but you can add honey to taste after straining out the sloes if
you must.

Sip a glass with the first sun of spring, while feeling glad that the
long, hungry winter is behind you at last.

The system of townland fines was introduced in 1783 and brought fully into force in 1806. It punished entire communities for the crimes of one or two residents. The new law stated that if a still was found anywhere on the land then the entire town or parish would be liable for a fine of up to £60. It was a hugely draconian measure, an unfair system, and it led to even greater animosity towards the revenue officers. It also allowed the gaugers even greater opportunity for extortion, as they could threaten to plant a still for themselves to find in any place at any time. The residents had no way to protect themselves from this kind of corruption.

After the gaugers imposed a townland fine, the job of collecting went to a separate person, the local fine-collector. Their job was to seize cattle, sheep, horses, even furniture from any residents of the townland until either the fine was paid – which the residents could rarely afford to do – or until they raised sufficient funds to cover it by selling the seized goods at auction. One fine-collector became particularly famous for his violence, cruelty and instability. He terrorised the people of Inishowen for twenty months before his conduct led to an enquiry and his dismissal. His name was Robert Newman.

As Newman's reputation spread throughout the county, many tried to escape his abuse by cooperating with him; but that wasn't enough to ensure safety. He was paranoid and distrustful, as well as completely uncaring about whether his source would be revealed to the unhappy locals. John

Gwynne had been assisting Newman for some time, negotiating with his customers at his grocer's shop to collect both fines and assurances that they would cease distilling. But when Newman received information about a nearby still, he accused Gwynne of betraying him. He abducted Gwynne from his house and forced him to ride along with him to the seizure in full view of his neighbours. As they passed, Newman told the neighbours that the information about the location of the still had come from Gwynne, which was not true. Luckily Gwynne must have been well known and trusted locally, as he doesn't seem to have suffered any serious reprisals.

John Colhoun was not so lucky. He was a middleman who leased a large portion of land in Donagh and then let it to small farmers on short leases, so it is likely that he would not have been well liked to begin with. When his parish was hit with a series of townland fines he approached Newman and offered to lead him to the places where his tenants had hidden their cattle, as they often hid them to prevent them from being seized. After several seizures had been made, Newman selected one cow, tied a rein for it and demanded that Colhoun personally walk it to the Carndonagh pound. He threatened him with a pistol and told him, 'You rascal, if you do not lead her I will blow your brains out! And I never fired at a man that I did not either kill or wound him.' Once Colhoun left with the cow, Newman proceeded to his house and seized two of his own cows, as well as ensuring that all of his tenants knew who had informed on their hiding places. Three weeks later, three of Colhoun's outhouses were burned down.

In an attempt to work with his tenants to clear the rest of the fines and avoid attracting more of their anger, Colhoun then went to Newman to get a statement of the remaining fines owed. He agreed with him the amounts he and his tenants would pay, and took the demand back to his townland. He managed to get his tenants to pay their shares, but on the appointed day Newman simply did not show up to collect. Colhoun's tenants accused him of inventing the agreement to extort money from them for himself. They burned down all of his remaining outhouses.

For some reason, Colhoun continued to throw himself on Newman's clearly non-existent mercy. He paid all of the fines himself on the condition that Newman would send the army to help him recoup his tenant's shares. With all the money that he was owed already in hand, Newman never had any intention of sending anyone to help the middleman collect. Broke and with most of his farm already destroyed by his own tenants, Colhoun was forced to leave the area in disgrace.

Newman acted just as dishonestly after the seizures as he did during them. The owners of seized goods were supposed to get an opportunity to buy their livestock back at market value before they were put up for auction, but Newman often refused to sell them at any price.

Neil McCandless was visiting his brother George when Newman came and seized George's cattle. Newman also took Neil's horse, which he had ridden to his brother's house. Neil went to Derry to retrieve his horse and offered to buy it back, even though it should not have been part of the seizure in the first place. Newman told him that it was worth £10 but that he would not sell it back, and continued to refuse to sell it even when Neil McCandless offered him £15. A few days later the hapless farmer noticed that the horse was gone from the pound, without even going up for auction where he might have had a chance of winning her back. He eventually discovered that Newman had illegally sold the mare to another Revenue employee for a pitiful £2 10s. Given how much more the horse would have fetched at auction, Newman could only have sold it so cheaply out of spite.

When Neil's brother George came to try to retrieve his cattle, he had even less luck than Neil. Things seemed promising at first: Newman offered him all six cows for £8. Things started to go wrong later when Newman upped the price to £12, apparently on the advice of the auctioneer. Still, George pulled out his purse and paid the £12, at which point Newman grabbed the purse and emptied it onto the desk. He took the £12, along with everything else he found, and then simply told the farmer to go home without his money or his cattle. Fearing Newman's violent temper, and with no hope of proving the theft in court against the might of the revenue service, all George McCandless could do was plead with Newman. He told him that he had no way of getting home, causing Newman to disdainfully throw him two ten-penny pieces to cover his expenses.

If you had been luckier than the McCandlesses and had managed to hold on to your cattle as well as your poitín, you could have tried a luxuriously rich drink made with poitín and butter which was described by Isaac Butler on his travels through some of the richer areas near Dublin.

HOT BUTTERED POITÍN: THE ORIGINAL

To make it the more agreeable they fill an iron pot with ys spirit, putting sugar, mint and butter and when it hath seethed for some time they fill their square cans which they call Meathers and this drink out then to each other. What is surprising they will drink it to Intoxication and are never sick after it neither doth it impair their health.

Isaac Butler, Journey Through Fermanagh *(1760)*

THE ALCHEMIST'S VERSION

25g butter

25g sugar

50ml water

2 sprigs mint

100ml whiskey

It may not be the traditional method, but the only way I can find to combine these ingredients without producing a horrible oily

*slick across the top of the whiskey is to make a butterscotch from
the sugar and butter before adding the whiskey.*

*Melt the butter and sugar in a small pan over a gentle heat.
Once the sugar has dissolved, turn the heat up to full and let
the mixture bubble until it just starts to turn brown. Next, while
stirring constantly, add the water a teaspoon at a time until
you have added it all. Turn the heat down very low, toss in the
mint and let the flavour from the mint infuse into the sauce for
5–10 minutes before removing the stalks again. Finally, add the
whiskey a teaspoon at a time until it is fully incorporated. Even
with this method, the butter will eventually separate out once the
mixture cools, so be sure to drink it immediately.*

*Serve in a mether cup, if you have one. This traditional cup is
four-sided, with a handle on each side, and was designed to be
passed around and shared. Alternatively, you could serve it in a
mug with only one handle, which would force you to drink it all
yourself. Poor you.*

Even innocent bystanders were in trouble when Robert
Newman was around. When John McMonigle was walking
along the highway, minding his own business, Newman
commanded him to stop two passing horses carrying sacks
of potatoes. McMonigle ignored him, rightly assuming that
the matter was none of his business and that Newman had

no power to command him to assist. Newman was explosively angry, and he hit McMonigle with the flat of his sword while ordering the bemused soldiers to stab him. Then, when the soldiers refused, he chased the poor man with a revolver, only letting him escape when he leapt into a large ditch filled with water to hide.

On another occasion Newman commandeered Neal McFarren's horse and cart to carry off a load of flax and barley. Even though the cart was filled with barley and the party made frequent stops at inns, Newman refused to feed the man or the horse for the whole of the two days that it took to transport the load. McFarren confronted Newman about the way that they had been treated when they stopped at one of the inns, but Newman just grabbed him and threw him out the inn door and down a flight of steps. While McFarren was not seriously hurt by his fall, the horse apparently died from its mistreatment just a few days later. They'd had to whip the starving animal too hard to get it to keep up with the rest of the party.

Other bystanders were at risk simply for doing their jobs. The Foyle bridge toll collector, Phillip Molloy, was just trying to collect the normal toll for crossing the bridge from Newman and his party. Newman accused him of intentionally delaying them and of conspiring with the local poitín makers to give them time to escape. Apparently deciding that this imagined slight by the toll keeper was more important than the seizures they had been on their way to make, Newman took the toll keeper prisoner and forced him to ride with them for an hour. They went directly to the guardhouse where the area's head toll farmer lived and Newman handed him a list of charges against his employee, then dismissed them both and went back to his seizure. Although the experience was alarming, the toll keeper escaped unharmed, and so did better than most of those that encountered Newman.

Given how badly he treated even innocent passers-by, it should come as no surprise that Newman was excessively violent with the people whose homes he was supposed to be searching. His violent ways were also passed on to his deputies. Some were probably violent men just like him, but others simply knew how he wanted things done and that they would be in danger themselves if they defied his wishes. When his assistant Edward Moriarty fired a warning shot at shopkeeper James Miller, Newman was angry that his assistant had not gone further, even though Miller was surrounded by five of his children and holding a nine-month-old baby in his arms. When Newman arrived he shouted at Moriarty, 'Damn your soul, Edward! Why did you not shoot the bugger!?' James Miller's brother Robert tried to object, but quickly found the fine-collector shoving him with a pistol in each hand, telling him that he should have been shot as well.

Even Anne Brumhall, an eighty-year-old widow, was shown no mercy when two of Newman's assistants arrived to seize her cattle to pay a new townland fine. Her cattle weren't enough to cover the fine, and they demanded that she tell them where they could find cattle belonging to the neighbouring distillers. She refused to tell them, fearing reprisals, and they stripped her house bare, even taking the bed from underneath her sick daughter.

No one attempted to take legal action against Newman for his crimes, as they knew that the Revenue would use their combination of money and influence to ensure that it was futile, just as they had at the Ballyshannon trial. It was a local priest, Edward Chichester, who finally brought about Newman's downfall. Chichester had originally been a supporter of the Revenue, assisting them in shutting down the stills, which he thought were a threat to the moral and economic health of the district. It was only after he personally intervened to stop the people of Urris from firing on the Revenue, and as a result saw a young man hung for the shots that had been fired at him, that he decided the revenue service had gone too far.

As his first act of defiance, he dined with the commanding officer of an army unit which was supposed to be accompanying Newman on a raid the following day, and persuaded him that the inhabitants were planning a general uprising and that they would all fight any army presence with their very lives. They would be too much for just one unit to handle, and he would put his men in danger if they went on the raid. The army stayed in the barracks the next day, sending only a short note to the fine-collector.

However, it was the long and detailed letter of complaint that Chichester sent to the revenue service that finally triggered the enquiry leading to Newman's dismissal. The letter contained detailed reports that he had collected of dozens of incidents of violence and abuse of power, along with dates and the names of witnesses. Since Chichester was both a clergyman and the brother of a major landowner, they had to take his complaints seriously and could not simply dismiss them out of hand. They had also had concerns for a while about Newman's conduct and, more importantly to them, about his submitted expenses.

Robert Newman never faced charges for his crimes, but he was dismissed from the service and forced to repay £892 in erroneous expenses. His name never appears in the records again, and so what happened to him after his dismissal remains a mystery. Perhaps he met with a disgruntled former customer somewhere quiet late one night, when he no longer had the army at his beck and call.

In 1819 the draconian townland fines law was finally repealed, replaced with a £100 fine for possession of illicit spirits. In the same year the revenue police were established, a new force dedicated solely to the extermination of illicit distilling. The pay was poor, the work dangerous and there were initially no bonuses for captures; and so the job attracted retired soldiers, often ones who were incapable of doing the work through age or injury, and thugs who wanted legal permission to bully and intimidate.

The revenue police ended up with a reputation even worse than the gaugers' had been, and they also had a much worse relationship with other agencies. The coastguard, in particular, resented this upstart agency who attempted to make demands of them when they were busy with their own fight against smuggling. They refused on numerous occasions to provide the revenue police with the transport they needed to make seizures on islands off the coast.

When the Dunfanaghy detachment was refused coast-guard help to make a seizure on Inishbofin in 1826, they commandeered a local boat instead. It ended up wrecked off the coast, with eleven prisoners, in addition to the men of the revenue police, in the water. The coastguard refused to come to their rescue. For a short time in 1832 the Gortahork coastguard were forced by their superiors into helping the Sligo detachment to reach Inishmurray, but they were worse than no help at all. The coastguard cutter had to pass by the island on its way from the station to collect the revenue police, giving the islanders plenty of warning that a raid was coming and time to ensure that stills and their produce were thoroughly hidden.

While violence and confrontation were common, there were some who kept their stills concealed rather than fight for them – possibly many more, since only the ones that were discovered were recorded. In Killybegs, a secret room was found hidden inside the gable roof of a farmhouse with a flue attached to the kitchen chimney to hide the smoke, and elsewhere Andy Bealy was found to be ferment-ing 380 gallons of pot ale inside a hollow stack of peats at the end of his house. Meanwhile, in Inishowen, the Grants had built an entire false floor in their bedroom to cover the malting floor concealed below.

When a colonel was finally appointed to take charge of the revenue police and instil some order in 1836 he said of the current force that 'the law has given to this corps powers stronger and more summary than to any other armed force in the empire . . . yet . . . they have in too many instances converted their arms into instruments of vengeance in private quarrels, or used them without orders from their officers, upon a slight appearance of obstruction in their duties'.

He was determined to turn the force around, and removed more than two-thirds of the current officers within the first year for reasons including 'no longer being capable of performing', being 'intoxicated while on duty from a seized cask', severely wounding a fellow officer in the head with a rifle, 'troubling the board with his private affairs', gross negligence, and finally one officer who, 'instead of destroying a distillery, allowed it to finish, had portion of it, and had the remainder carried to the barracks for the use of the men'.

The new force was certainly an improvement on the shambles that had come before it, but when the potato blight began in 1845, mere poitín-making ceased to be the most important crisis in Ireland. The force found that they no longer had the interest of the government, and with the loss of interest came a lack of recording. Peace at last for the poitín-makers, perhaps, but also a lack of stories for me to tell. The revenue police were quietly disbanded in 1857 as militant nationalism was increasing, and with the eventual dawning of independence, any stills that may or may not have remained in operation have ceased to be within the scope of this book. There may still be poitín coming from the worms on the coasts of Mayo and Donegal, but anything they produce is now pure Irish spirit, and none of Britain's business.

CHAPTER FIVE

WORSE THINGS HAPPEN AT SEA

Customs duty – a charge on anything passing in or out of a country or city-state – is one of the oldest forms of taxation, and one of the easiest to collect (at least when no one is actively trying to avoid it). The duty goes all the way back to Athens in the first century BC, and smuggling of one kind of another is as old as the tax.

It was in 1206 that King John created the first English national service to collect for the crown, although customs was charged locally by some port towns before that date. During the centuries that followed, taxes on imports and exports waxed and waned, and different agencies enforced them in a variety of ways. However, customs duty was only collected at major ports, and little or no attention was paid to small ships arriving elsewhere along the coast. So long as a decent amount of money was coming in, it didn't matter if a little more slipped past uncollected. That all changed in 1614, when the export of wool was temporarily banned in order to shield the English textile industry from competition.

With a lucrative trade handed to them overnight, wool smugglers, known as 'owlers', started to turn professional. They formed gangs and became such a trouble to the authorities that in 1661 the illegal export of wool became punishable by death. Far from stopping the problem, this drove the smugglers to become more cunning, more organised and more violent. The smuggler of legend – the romantic outlaw, pitting his wits against the men of the Revenue – was born.

But if smuggling was still about exporting wool, what does that have to do with spirits? The shift from export to import smuggling happened gradually, as taxes on tea, tobacco and spirits were increased by leaps and bounds in order to fund a series of wars during the eighteenth and nineteenth centuries. The War of Jenkins' Ear, the Seven Years' War, the War of American Independence and finally the Napoleonic Wars all came with big hikes in duty and, since the enemy was most often France, complete bans on the import of brandy. Tea, tobacco and spirits were the main smuggled commodities. The popularity of tea and tobacco fluctuated in response to the levels of tax imposed – duty was known to climb as high as five times the original value of the product, before being periodically cut to discourage smuggling – but the smuggling of spirits never went out of fashion.

At first, the only enforcers were the riding officers, who were based only on land. One of the favoured means of defying them was for a big foreign trading vessel to anchor itself just off the coast as a floating market. The riding officer had no chance of catching the multiple small boats, mostly local fishing boats, which would sail out to make purchases, and he had no support on the sea to drive off the traders. That changed with the introduction of the Waterguard in 1700, and the Hovering Act eighteen years later made the very act of 'hovering' near the shore with no legal purpose punishable by the seizure and destruction of the vessel. The huge floating markets were driven off, and smaller boats had to make the entire trip to suppliers abroad. So began a cat-and-mouse game with ever-increasing stakes, as the law got harsher and enforcement got tighter. It would last well over a hundred years.

In the early 1700s, landings tended to happen on open beaches, the operation protected by brute force rather than secrecy; making landings at night was the only concession to concealment. A boat would simply sail up onto an open beach where a large force would be waiting to receive the goods in caravan, while the protective batsmen stood by with wooden clubs in case of trouble. These landings took place all over the country. They were mostly local affairs for local markets with between fifty and 200 men; but in the counties of Kent and Sussex, which were close to the hungry London market and just a short hop across the channel from France, organised gangs grew up to perform landings on an industrial scale. The big smuggling gangs were named after their headquarters – often towns that were many miles inland. Since their power grew from their control of overland routes and their ability to transport goods to larger markets, it was at the heart of these routes that they had their bases.

The village of Hawkhurst, for example, is fifteen miles from the coast. It was a key point on the route from the landing beaches to the depots south of London, such as Stockwell, where merchants and middlemen from the city would attend open-air auctions of smuggled goods. From there, the merchants would often mix the smuggled spirits in with smaller quantities of legal ones. A little creative book-keeping and the Revenue were none the wiser, but profits were significantly better. This meant that smuggled brandy would have found its way into the hands of many important and famous people without their knowledge – not that many would have minded if they had known. Perhaps the 'punch' so carefully described by Charles Dickens in a letter to his friend's sister was made with a drop of the naughty stuff? Let's assume that it was. Dickens was as good at writing recipes as he was at writing novels.

CHARLES DICKENS' PUNCH: THE ORIGINAL

*Peel into a very strong common basin (which may be broken,
in case of accident, without damage to the owner's peace or
pocket) the rinds of three lemons, cut very thin, and with as little
as possible of the white coating between the peel and the fruit,
attached. Add a double-handfull of lump sugar (good measure),
a pint of good old rum, and a large wine glass full of brandy — if
it not be a large claret-glass say two. Set this on fire, by filling a
warm silver spoon with the spirit, lighting the contents at a wax
taper, and pouring them gently in. Let it burn for three or four
minutes at least, stirring it from time to time. Then extinguish
it by covering the basin with a tray, which will immediately put
out the flame. Then squeeze in the juice of three lemons, add a
quart of boiling water. Stir up the whole well, cover it up for five
minutes, and stir again.*

*At this crisis (having skimmed off the lemon pips with a spoon)
you may taste. If not sweet enough, add sugar to your liking,
but observe that it will be a little sweeter presently. Pour the
whole thing into a jug, tie a leather or coarse cloth over the top,
so as to exclude the air completely, and stand it in a hot oven
ten minutes, or on a hot stove one quarter of an hour. Keep it
until it comes to the table in a warm place near the fire but not
too hot.*

Letter from Charles Dickens to Mrs F. (18 January 1847)

THE ALCHEMIST'S VERSION

Zest and juice of 3 lemons
As many brown sugar cubes as you can hold in both
hands (or about 170g of loose demerara)
450ml rum (if you can get hold of a dark overproof rum, that would
be ideal; otherwise any navy style will do fine. Do not use white rum)
250ml brandy (Dickens would have used the
best VSOP, but a VS cognac will do)
1 litre boiling water

If you're not hosting an entire party, you can halve the quantities; the modern tolerance for alcohol is not what it once was.

Use a stainless steel saucepan with tight-fitting lid, or failing that, a heatproof bowl and plate, but be careful. Be sure that the handle of the saucepan is oven-proof, and don't use one with a non-stick coating.

Place the lemon zest into the pan and add the sugar, rum and brandy. Making sure that you're away from anything flammable, use a tablespoon to take a spoonful of the mixture and use a match or a lighter to first warm it, then light it. Slowly pour the lit spirit into the bowl to flambé the whole thing, and wait for four minutes. Put the lid on the pan using an oven glove and give it a moment for the flames to go out. Add the juice of the lemons and the boiling water and stir well, cover and leave for five minutes, then stir again.

At this point, test the sweetness and add more sugar if you want it. Put the lid back on. The pan needs to be well sealed or you'll lose a lot of the alcohol in the next stage, so if there are gaps or steam holes, it will help to put a layer of foil over the pan before putting the lid on. Put the pan in an oven and cook at 180°C for ten minutes. You can then either drink it immediately, or turn the oven down to its lowest setting and leave to keep warm until needed — but strain out the lemon rinds first if you're leaving it for more than an hour or two.

Ladle into cups and drink while reading some friends your latest work: either one of the greatest works of fiction of all time, or a rambling moral polemic, depending on your point of view.

Hawkhurst was the base of the Hawkhurst gang who became one of the most infamous organisations – not because they were anything special in terms of size, influence, professionalism or even violence, but because they were caught and put on trial as a lesson to others. The first recorded mention of the Hawkhurst gang is in 1735, when a convoy run by the gang was ambushed by customs officers acting on an informant's tip-off. The gang escaped that time, but only after one of their number had been shot and killed. They are next spotted in the record in 1740, forcibly retrieving a wagon of tea that had been seized by the authorities. In 1746 they got into a fight with

another gang from nearby Wingham when a joint operation went wrong; the Hawkhursts wounded seven of the
other gang and stole forty of their horses. But the incident
that made them famous – or infamous – happened the
following year.

A cutter called the *Three Brothers* was making a run from
Guernsey on behalf of the Hawkhurst gang when it was
seized by the revenue service. The crew escaped, but the
ship was taken and the cargo stored in the customs house in
Poole. When they heard the news, the gang decided to take
their cargo back, and headed down to Poole with a group of
thirty armed men. On arrival, they were frustrated to find
a sloop-of-war moored by the customs house with swivel
guns aimed towards it. The gang came close to abandoning
the retrieval before they realised that as the boat went down
with the tide, the customs house would eventually pass out
of range of the guns.

They broke into the customs house and took back their
tea without any further problems (although they had to
leave the brandy behind because it was too bulky to carry),
and set off back to their headquarters. The whole operation would have been a flawless success if one member of
the gang, John Diamond, had not spotted an old friend in
the watching crowd as they passed through Fordingbridge.
He stopped and gave his friend, local shoemaker Daniel
Chater, a small bag of tea 'for old times' sake'.

When a £500 reward was posted for information about
the gang a few days later, Daniel did not betray them, but he

did start boasting locally about his connection to the daring smugglers. Word eventually got back to the authorities, and Chater was arrested and compelled to identify Diamond to the local justice of the peace. Chater had to be taken to the magistrate's house to testify, and for the journey he was given only one escort: an elderly customs official named William Galley. This was to prove a fatal mistake.

Chater and Galley found themselves lost soon after leaving town, and stopped at the White Hart Inn to ask for directions. The landlady, who was a confederate of the smugglers, kept the two men well supplied with drink while she called the gang in to deal with them. When the smugglers arrived, they continued plying Chater and Galley with drink until they fell asleep, at which point the gang searched them and found a letter they were carrying to the justice of the peace, telling him their intentions. By this time, smuggling was a capital offence, and the whole gang was faced with the gallows if they were identified, so this letter sealed the pair's fate.

Later, at the trial, it was claimed that many of the gang wanted simply to transport the two men to France or keep them captive – but one man, William Jackson, was determined to make an example of them. He took charge of the situation, putting on his spurs and waking Chater and Galley by spurring their faces. He had them whipped, then seated them together on a horse with their legs tied underneath its belly. The gang continued to whip them as the horse was led on to the next safe house at the Red Lion Inn, but eventually they were so badly injured that they could no longer hold on. They slid round the horse until they were hanging underneath its belly, where it kicked them in the head as it walked. Finally they were removed from the horse and reseated with each of them riding pillion behind one of the smugglers. The rest of the gang only stopped whipping them when the men carrying them complained that they were also being hit.

By the time the group arrived at the Red Lion Inn, William Galley appeared to be dead. The smugglers chained Daniel Chater up in the turf store and, after nightfall, took Galley's body out into some nearby woodland to bury him. When his corpse was eventually found he was standing nearly upright, covering his eyes with his hand. Many believed that he may only have been unconscious, and that the gang had buried him alive. The decision about what to do with Chater took longer, but after he had spent three days chained in the turf store without food or drink, they decided that he must be disposed of. Benjamin Tapner, the first of the gang to go in, slashed his face, blinding him and almost cutting off his nose. Then they rode out with him to Harris's Well, several miles away. After trying to hang him with a rope that they found was too short to do the job, they threw him – still alive – down the well, and flung stones down after him until the noise stopped.

The scale of the violence shocked the locals, and an anonymous letter led to the discovery of William Galley's body. Another letter named gang member William Steele as the murderer. When Steele was arrested, he turned on the other participants and named them in exchange for his own freedom. He also revealed the names of twenty-six of the men who had gone to Poole. The murderers, it turned out, were not from the Hawkhurst gang at all, but from another Chichester group who sometimes worked with them. They had not even been involved in the original crime, but had still been determined to make an example of Chater and Galley for all potential informers.

The extreme violence shown towards informers was partly a response to a 1746 law that allowed the names of any known smugglers to be published in the *London Gazette*. Any man who was 'gazetted' and did not turn himself in within four weeks was immediately sentenced to death in his absence, and a £500 reward was offered for information leading to his capture. This was a life-changing amount of money at a time when a labourer would be lucky to earn £15 in a year, and so smugglers lived in constant fear of informers. They believed that such a great reward, and such a great risk to themselves, required a level of violence that would provoke fear equal to the temptation.

A special assize was held in 1749 to try the murderers of Galley and Chater. Six justices were brought down from London, as it was felt their local counterparts might be in league with the smugglers. Five men were found guilty of the murders, and sentenced to hang and to have their bodies gibbeted – publicly hung in chains as an example to others – after death. One of these, William Jackson, escaped the noose by dying in his cell the night before the execution. Two other men were found guilty of being accessories to the murder and were also sentenced to hang, but not to be gibbeted.

Of the other nineteen men who had taken part in the expedition to Poole, two more turned informer to save their own skins; seven were executed as smugglers; and eight were executed for the unrelated murders of Thomas Carswell and Michael Bath, revenue officers who had been killed in previous skirmishes with the gang. So many losses effectively brought the Hawkhurst gang to an end, and 1748 also saw a drop-off in smuggling in general as the War of the Austrian Succession came to an end and duties were dropped. Thirty years later they were once again sky-high and smuggling activity came to a second peak, with new Kent gangs formed to take advantage of the trade.

Although the big gangs in Kent and Sussex lost the support of the public with the scale of their violence, smugglers elsewhere could still count on the help and the silence of the community. This was demonstrated when a landing near Fowey in Cornwall was interrupted by two coastguards. The smugglers knocked one unconscious, but the other managed to arrest five gang members before they could get away. However, when the case went to trial and they were charged with 'assisting others in landing and carrying away prohibited goods, some being armed with offensive weapons', the jury acquitted them on the flimsy pretext that they did not consider bats to be offensive weapons. Cases like this were part of the reason that many accused smugglers were taken away to London to be tried at the Old Bailey.

When eleven smugglers were being held in Dover jail, the locals didn't even wait for a trial. They rioted and over-ran the jail where, unable to get through the doors, they literally tore the roof apart. The Mayor of Dover arrived and tried to read the Riot Act, but soon gave up when the crowd on the roof started throwing tiles at him. Once the hole was big enough for them to get through, the prisoners were lifted out and carried away to the Red Cow Inn to have their chains removed. The riot continued for some time even after the smugglers left, and the jail was damaged so far beyond repair that it had to be rebuilt. The whole incident lives on in a local folk song called 'The Breaking of Dover Gaol'.

Smugglers could also often count on the locals to assist them by signalling whether it was safe to land. Windmills were a common choice for signalling, with the sails set in an upright cross to show that landing was safe and in a diagonal X to warn of danger. Where there were a num-ber of mills within sight of each other, a signal could be passed from one to another very quickly. There was such a good signalling line on the Norfolk Broads that it was said a warning could travel from the windmill closest to the customs house in Yarmouth up the coast to Horsey in just fifteen minutes – twice as fast as a man on horseback could make the journey, even at a gallop.

Other daylight signalling methods included the posi-tioning of cows or sheep in meaningful ways, or particular people passing down the shore. On Looe Island a farmer would ride along the coast road on his distinctive white horse if the coast was clear, but if there was trouble he would walk and lead the horse. At night, when men were waiting on the beach, a flash from the muzzle of a pistol or musket loaded only with gunpowder was the favoured signal, and could be answered with a matching signal from the ship.

But the signal didn't need to be so near – the darkness of the coast, in the days before electric lighting, meant that a small light could be seen for miles. A lantern might be placed in a window a long way inland and still act as a good signal. Of course, if smugglers could see your light for miles, so could the authorities, which meant that the light needed to be pointed as directly out to sea as possible. Some of the most fascinating smugglers' artefacts that survive today are the spout lanterns. They were made of solid metal on three sides, while the fourth had a hollow tube as long as a forearm in order to point a beam of light straight out over the water.

While in some areas smugglers had only a few trusted confidantes, in others the distinction between the smugglers and the rest of the population hardly existed. In Cornwall – a county where it is never possible to be more than twenty miles from the sea – it was common for an entire village to be involved in the business of smuggling. Most villages relied on the seasonal fishing industry, so when the tax on salt was raised so high that pilchard fishermen couldn't afford the salt they needed to preserve their fish for winter, smuggling was deemed necessary to survival. Of course, once started, they didn't just bring salt for themselves – they also brought tea, tobacco and brandy for sale. A little brandy kept back before the rest was sold could be used to preserve a little luxury or two to last yourself through the winter as well.

PEACHES PRESERVED IN BRANDY: THE ORIGINAL

A nice way to preserve Peaches

Put your peaches in boiling water, just give them a scald, but don't let them boil, take them out and put them in cold water, then dry them in a sieve, and put them in long wide mouth bottles: To half a dozen peaches take a quarter of a pound of sugar, clarify it, pour it over your peaches, and fill the bottles with brandy. Stop them close, and keep them in a close place.

Hannah Glasse, The Art of Cookery Made Plain and Easy *(1747)*

THE ALCHEMIST'S VERSION

6 peaches

100g sugar

½ bottle of brandy (you probably won't need it all, but better to have too much than too little and drink the rest)

First, find a jar big enough to fit your peaches — a large Kilner jar is ideal. Cut a small cross in the base of each peach with a sharp knife, put them in a bowl and cover them with boiling water. Leave them for 10–15 minutes and then tip out the boiling water (being careful not to lose the peaches) and replace it with cold water. While the peaches sit in the cold water, put the sugar into a small pan with 100ml of water and place on a low heat, stirring constantly until the sugar has dissolved. Take the syrup off the heat, tip the peaches into a sieve and leave both to sit until the peaches have stopped dripping and the syrup is cool. Tip your peaches into the jar, add the syrup and top up with brandy until the peaches are completely covered. Put the lid on the jar and leave in a cool, dark place for at least a month.

These preserved brandy peaches are great on desserts, and as a bonus, you have peach brandy left over when all the peaches are gone. Don't drink it straight from the jar, no matter how tempting it is — at least, not while anyone is looking.

In the Cornish village of Polperro, the customs officer knew how the other locals felt about smuggling, and he knew when to look the other way. But in 1794, when the Supervisor of the Excise himself arrived with two other officers and a platoon of fourteen soldiers to make a dawn raid, he had no choice but to cooperate. The men had no difficulty locating and breaking into a cellar where, as the information they were acting on had promised, over 200 kegs of brandy were stored. When it came to removing the casks, however, they had a problem: most of the town had come out to stop them. Over a hundred men had gathered, and many were armed with sticks or muskets. Some had even lifted a swivel gun (a small cannon) down from the deck of a ship, and were aiming it at the door to the cellar. After a short confrontation, the Revenue and their soldiers were forced to leave without their prize.

The people of Polperro would come together again to protect their own after an unfortunate incident in 1799 brought the force of the law down hard on their community. A Polperro ship, the *Lottery*, was returning from a run to Guernsey on Boxing Day 1798 when a small customs boat drew alongside and unfurled its official blue flag. The crew of the *Lottery* fired on the customs boat. The three musket shots they fired were probably intended as a warning, but one of them hit an officer in the head, killing him instantly. The *Lottery* crew cut their anchor cable and took off for Polperro, unaware that they had killed an officer. When they learned the news, the men responsible were hidden in the town – but the ship, which would have been identified by the surviving officers, had nowhere to hide and had to continue plying the smuggling route to Guernsey.

Half the cargo had already been delivered to Plymouth for the Christmas celebrations, and the inhabitants would have been happily making their way through large quantities of smuggled brandy, tea, tobacco, sugar and spice, completely unaware of the violence that had been involved in bringing the goods to their doors. Many Christmas drinks were the same as everyday drinks, just consumed in larger quantities – but one was special to the season: the wassail, which would be offered to groups of wassailers at every door as they made their way around town. Although the tradition was ancient, the recipe changed over time. This recipe, written in 1827 as a record of how it was 'formerly prepared', is close to the way it would have been enjoyed in Plymouth as the *Lottery* crew fled for their lives. I've made a few extra tweaks to bring it more in line with some older recipes and mentions.

WASSAIL: THE ORIGINAL

Put into a bowl half a pound of Lisbon sugar; pour on it one pint of warm beer; grate a nutmeg and some ginger into it: add four glasses of sherry and five additional pints of beer; stir it well; sweeten it to your taste: let it stand covered up two or three hours, then put three or four slices of bread cut thin and toasted brown into it, and it is fit for use . . . The Wassail Bowl, or Wassail Cup, was formerly prepared in nearly the same way as present, excepting that roasted apples, or crab apples, were introduced instead of toasted bread.

R. Cook, Oxford Night Caps: A Collection of Receipts for Making Various Beverages (1827)

THE ALCHEMIST'S VERSION

4 large cooking apples

300g sugar

50g butter

250ml brandy

1 inch piece of fresh ginger, peeled and chopped fine

½ a whole nutmeg (or ½ tsp ground nutmeg)

6 pints of dark ale or cider (or 3 litres)

First remove the cores from the apples and stand them up in a small roasting dish. Weigh out 75g of the sugar and put a quarter of that sugar, plus a quarter of the butter, into each apple. Cover the dish with foil and bake at 200°C for half an hour, or until the apples are almost falling apart. Meanwhile, put the remaining 225g of sugar into a large bowl with the ginger, grate over the nutmeg and stir it all up together. Heat one pint (500ml) of the ale or cider until it is just starting to steam, then add it to the bowl and stir well until the sugar dissolves. Add the rest of the ale or cider, as well as the brandy, cover with a clean tea towel and leave to sit for two hours while the apples are also cooling.

When your guests arrive, add the apples to the bowl and give it a good stir. Little fluffy bits of apple will float to the surface — these give the drink its older name, lambswool.

Share with your neighbours and enjoy by a roaring yule fire, blissfully unaware of the terrible things happening elsewhere.

The *Lottery* managed to keep going for four more months before it was captured, and in all that time no one from Polperro claimed the £200 reward offered for information about the shooting. However, when the ship's luck finally ran out and it was finally spotted by the revenue making another run to Guernsey there was one man aboard, Roger Toms, who had also been present during the shooting. He agreed to testify in order to save his own life. Three men were arrested, and Toms was made a member of the crew of a Revenue cutter for his own protection while he waited to be called as a witness.

If he'd stayed on the cutter, he might have been safe; but he was tricked into a secret rendezvous with his wife, then abducted and shipped to Guernsey. It took the customs service a year to locate him again since their authority on the island was a little shaky, but eventually he was found. Thomas Potter was subsequently convicted of the revenue officer's murder, and sentenced to hang; the other two men who had been arrested with him were both convicted of smuggling and sentenced to two years' hard labour. Roger Toms, now greatly in fear for his life, knew he could never return to Polperro, so he was given a job as a turnkey in Newgate for his own protection – which, ironically, meant that he spent the rest of his life in prison, albeit on the other side of the bars.

By this time, with France having declared war in 1793, Britain was in the midst of a twenty-year period of conflict; the Revolutionary Wars would eventually become the

Napoleonic Wars, not that the change of name meant much to the average citizen. The fighting provided smugglers with both new opportunities and new dangers. Traditional smuggling ports lined up to register vessels as privateers – licensed pirates, preying on French merchant shipping in the name of the king. It was an excellent cover for sailing a large, heavily armed smuggling vessel near the coast of France, if you could afford the necessary Letters of Marque. There were also great gains to be made doing the actual privateering if luck was on your side; the crew was supposed to receive the proceeds from the sale of the ships and goods they captured, which could fetch as much as £10,000. But the profits could also end up being tied up in red tape for years, so a little smuggling on the side helped provide a stable income.

The war also needed bodies, and smugglers faced new danger from the press gangs since their excellent seafaring skills made them attractive navy recruits. The need for manpower was so great that an Act of Oblivion had been proclaimed in 1782, pardoning any smuggling offence if the offender entered the navy – or if you were not willing to enter the navy yourself, you could be pardoned any offence up to a £500 penalty if you found two others willing to enter on your behalf, and any offence at all if you found four. The proceeds of smuggling could easily buy a few men to take your place, leaving you with a clean record. Candidates would openly advertise their willingness to join for a fee in the papers, at a going rate of around £9 per man.

Nevertheless, the advantages the war brought to smugglers were outweighed by the problems it caused. As the threat of invasion by sea grew, the British government began building coastal defences that would repel both smugglers and invaders. A chain of 103 coastal guard towers, known as Martello towers, were erected along the coasts of Kent, Sussex, Essex and Suffolk, commanding a good view of the whole sea and coast. The Royal Military Canal was also dug, cutting off Romney Marsh from the mainland to prevent any ground troops who might be landed there from marching inland. It also effectively prevented the movement of contraband over land from a series of popular landing places along the maze-like coast of the marsh. Although the canal was fordable in places, such spots were difficult to find; one group of smugglers drowned at Pett Levels when, pursued by the preventatives, they attempted to ford the canal in the wrong place.

When the war ended with Napoleon's defeat at Waterloo in 1815, returning soldiers started turning to smuggling to make a living. The government stepped up preventative efforts, using their new coastal defences against the smugglers. The Coastal Blockade was established to provide a constant guard over the whole coast from Sheerness to Beachy Head, day and night. It gradually expanded until it covered the whole of the Kent and Sussex coasts and employed almost 3,000 men, all of whom were sent to work in areas away from their homes to reduce collusion. The smugglers disposed of one or two of the new blockade men by removing the stones that they used to mark the cliff edges at night, and some others by more direct means; but more soon took their place. The blockade wasn't going anywhere, and smuggling techniques were going to have to adapt to the new regime. The era of open landings was at an end, and the time of tricks and sneaking began.

The old riding officers had often been amenable to taking bribes, as was obvious from the fortunes that many mysteriously acquired while on the job. (The riding officer at Herne during the 1730s managed to gain so much wealth that he qualified for a vote, something that was restricted to only the largest landowners.) But attempts to bribe the new blockade officers were trickier to arrange, simply because there were so many more of them, both on land and at sea. A group of smugglers at Rye harbour had succeeded in bribing the two land officers there only to have the HMS *Severn* unexpectedly arrive, leaving the officers with no choice but to let the ship help them capture the smugglers. The gang were so outraged that they reported the two officers for corruption.

Many ghost stories have their origin around this time – a good story could keep the superstitious away from a smugglers' hideout, and could also explain away any bumps and scrapes produced by handling kegs. The Palace House at Beaulieu, Hampshire was used as a warehouse by a group of smugglers who put on a regular show of otherworldly screams and clanking chains to keep alive the haunting rumours they had spread. Meanwhile, the vicar at Talland in Cornwall was said to be able to raise and lower the dead, and could often be seen in the graveyard at night swinging incense, surrounded by ghostly figures. The handy table tombs there could easily conceal four or five kegs each.

But the prize for the greatest ghost act must go to the man who earned himself the nickname 'Resurrection' Jackman for his funereal escapade. After he had been a thorn in their side for years, the Revenue had finally gathered enough evidence to try Jackman, and had come to arrest him. They were met by his tearful family at the door and told that he was dead. Being sensibly suspicious of such a convenient demise, two officers insisted on following the funeral cortege the next night as it made its way to Totnes for the burial of Jackman's unusually large coffin. It was a dark night and the men must have already been jumpy, because when they saw a hooded figure ride up on a black horse with an unnaturally pale face that looked just like Jackman's, they fled and did not return. 'Resurrection' Jackman had covered himself in flour, and gone out play his own ghost.

Vicars were often involved in local schemes; a vicar, knowing his congregation well, would usually accept that smuggling was one of the only ways they could make a living. The Reverend Patten of Whitstable even took a tithe from the proceeds of smuggling, as he would have from any profession. He turned in one band only because they refused to pay. The clergy's role was generally a passive one of helping by turning a blind eye – or, like the rector Phillip

Meadows in Suffolk, leaving the door to his stable open so that the smugglers could borrow his carriage. The cooperation of one vicar on the isle of Purbeck was inadvertently revealed when the ceiling of the knave gave way during a service, showering the audience with kegs. Meanwhile, at Hove, the parson seemed genuinely unaware of the use smugglers were making of his church. He had two parishes, Preston and St Andrews, and would preach at them on alternate Sundays; but when one week he mixed up his schedule and arrived at the wrong church, he found a congregation of kegs waiting for him in the pews.

There were plenty of other hiding places, apart from churches and graveyards. Pubs were obvious candidates, since they were often the final destination for much of the cargo. Some historic hiding places still survive as interesting features, such as the hidden shaft that runs all the way from the ground to the roof at the Spread Eagle pub in Witham, Essex. It once had no openings except on the roof, and smugglers would lower kegs down on ropes; but it now has a small window cut in at bar level, to show it off to visitors. In the Hastings Arms (in, unsurprisingly, Hastings, East Sussex), a keg could be installed underneath a window ledge on the first floor and connected by a pipe to a tap above the bar for discreet retailing. The last keg is still in place, although not in use.

Farms could also provide good storage places, such as basements with entrances concealed by stables or fireplaces. Both would be difficult for the Revenue to get to in a hurry if the fire was lit or the horse had a temper. The basement at Colne Farm had its entrance hidden behind a kiln, and the raid that uncovered it recovered eighty chests of tea, 140 ankers of brandy and 200 bales of tobacco. Haystacks and dungheaps might also be used to hide kegs, either directly or by masking access to an underground store. These arrangements could be perilous: the dung gave off large quantities of carbon dioxide as it fermented in the sun, and the gas could sink down and fill the store. When a group of smugglers opened up their own secret chamber beneath a dungheap in Coldfair Green, they didn't leave enough time for the gas to dissipate before they went down; all three men passed out, and two of them never woke again.

Such stories beg the question: after being soaked in the sea, brought to shore under a pile of fish, hauled up a cliff face and finally stashed underneath some warm dung for a few days, what would the brandy end up tasting like? Well, often not very good. In the West Country, the spoilt brandy that would sometimes find its way to customers earned the straightforward nickname 'stinky-booze'. But was a more positive outcome possible? The small casks used for smuggling exposed the brandy to a much greater surface area of wood, giving the ageing process a bit of a boost. A lot of salt water leaking in through the cheap and flimsy casks would be terrible, but just a hint of salt can be an excellent flavour-enhancer. Dung might not have much to contribute in the way of taste, but a little time in a sweet, fresh haystack might just allow some interesting grassy notes to creep in.

SMUGGLED BRANDY: THE ALCHEMIST'S VERSION

*200ml brandy (be optimistic about that rapid ageing
and use a VSOP cognac, or be more realistic and use
something cheap and a teaspoon of oak chips)
½ a handful of hay
½ tsp nam pla (Thai fish sauce)*

Put the brandy into a large sealable jar with the hay (and the oak chips, if using) and leave in a dark place for 2–3 days. Strain the mixture through a sieve or cheesecloth into a clean bottle, and add the nam pla.

Offer the brandy to your guests as the very best smuggled Crowlink. Compared to how bad it could have been, this really is the best.

Many caves have reputations as hiding places, but most of these are simply local lore; a brief exploration of the caves in question will often show they are too small, too noticeable or prone to flooding at high tide. There are, however, a few proven smugglers' caves. One, in Margate, was used in earlier times but had already been lost and passed into local legend by the mid 1700s. It was only rediscovered when a gardener fell through the roof while working on the garden behind Northumberland House in 1798. The rich, eccentric owner of the house, Francis Forster, immediately turned it into a smuggling museum, even as real smuggling continued just a short distance from his door. The many smugglers' tunnels that are rumoured to exist around the country are equally difficult to find, and even less likely to be real – the sheer amount of work that would have gone into building a tunnel, the noise and the spoil would all have attracted too much attention. However, there was one real tunnel discovered by the Revenue in Ramsgate. They estimated that it would have taken eighteen months to dig at a cost of £200, an outlay not many gangs could have afforded. It was rediscovered in 1954, when a bulldozer fell into it.

A pre-existing tunnel was made use of at Lymington, where a floodwater drain ran beneath the Angel Inn and down to the shore. It wasn't large enough for a person to get through even at a crawl, but the end of a rope could be passed down with the water flow and then a small keg drawn back up. Tunnels originally dug for other purposes were also used at Durlston Bay on the island of Purbeck. The local marble quarry was a perfect warren of tunnels and concealment crevices where the Revenue would be given the runaround until the contraband could be safely stashed. Workers could take it out from the stash as it was needed in the large spoil baskets that they carried out of quarry every day.

Hiding places were also needed on board ships, to disguise the illicit part of the cargo under a less profitable legitimate one. Some ships were built with a double hull, leaving space for contraband to be hidden between the inner hull and the outer one. Two that were built this way were the *Sally* out of Hastings and the ironically named *Good Intent*, which was eventually caught and found to be carrying 1,100 gallons of brandy. Ships were also built with hollow masts, spars and even oars. Barrels were constructed with false bottoms to conceal a quantity of brandy under a seemingly full barrel of drinking water. When the Revenue caught onto this trick and started probing water barrels to check their depth, the makers started to build the concealed compartment so that it tapered up the sides of the barrel, leaving the full depth of water in the middle.

Spirits were the most difficult contraband to hide because liquids always need to be contained, whereas tea and tobacco could sometimes be disguised in plain sight. Suppliers grew skilled at twisting tobacco into convincing ropes, available in a range of thicknesses and lengths to match the ships' rigging so that they could be stashed in a locker and explained away as spare rope in case of breakages.

Most boats would carry a mixture of different types of contraband, and having travelled across the sea together, these would soon be brought back together in the popular punches of the day. Punch was having a final fling before the late 1800s ushered the cocktail in to take its place. The brandy, sugar, tea and even sometimes the citrus fruits essential to making it would all have been smuggled at various times. No surviving recipes contain that other smuggling staple, tobacco, but I cannot believe that not one person who received their share of a shipment all together ever tried it. Perhaps they simply weren't willing to put their name to a recipe, just as no one writes up their teenage experiments with vodka, sweets and their mum's dishwasher.

TEA PUNCH: THE ORIGINAL

Take ½ pint good brandy
½ pint good rum
¼ pound of loaf sugar, dissolved in water
1 ounce best green tea
1 quart boiling water
1 large lemon

Infuse the tea in the water. Warm a silver or other metal bowl until hot to the touch; place in it the brandy, rum, sugar, and the juice of the lemon. The oil of the lemon peel should first be obtained by rubbing with a few lumps of the sugar. Set the contents of the bowl on fire; and while flaming, pour in the tea gradually, stirring with a ladle. It will continue to burn for some

*time, and should be ladled into glasses while in that condition. A
heated metal bowl will cause the punch to burn much longer than
if a china bowl is used.*

Jerry Thomas, Bartender's Guide *(1887 reprint)*

THE ALCHEMIST'S VERSION

*8 tsp green tea (Chinese gunpowder is best, but
8 teabags of any pure green will do)
2 tsp pipe tobacco (optional, for if you have
that naughty teenage feeling)
1 litre of water, hot but just below boiling
100g sugar
1 large lemon
250ml brandy (a good VS cognac is best)
250ml rum (navy style or a dark overproof
is best; never use white rum)*

*First put the tea (and the tobacco, if using) into a large teapot
or a jug. Add the hot water and leave to brew for 3–4 minutes.
Once the tea has brewed, put the sugar into a clean jug and add
the tea, passing it through a tea strainer. Stir until the sugar has
fully dissolved, and leave to cool.*

*Use a stainless-steel bowl to assemble the punch if you have one,
or a large ceramic bowl, like a mixing bowl, if not. Preheat it by
filling it with boiling water, leaving for a couple of minutes and
then emptying. Zest the lemon into the bowl and add the juice,*

*the brandy and the rum. Use a tablespoon to take a spoonful
of the liquid, making sure that you are well clear of anything
flammable, and heat the spoon with a match or lighter, then
light the spirit. Gradually pour the lit spirit into the bowl until
it catches, and then very slowly add the tea while stirring with a
ladle. If the tea is added carefully, the punch should stay alight.*

*Serve with a metal ladle into heatproof glasses while still alight,
but make sure that your guests remember to blow it out before
drinking it. Also, don't leave it lit too long in the glass: the rim
can get extremely hot, and burnt lips are no fun at all.*

The level of probing that the Revenue had to perform on
every boat to catch these tricks started to cause trouble.
Fishermen constantly complained that the sharp 'pricker'
used by the Revenue to check the nets for contraband was
causing damage and affecting their legitimate livelihood.
The tension between the fishermen and the Revenue led
to tragedy in 1821, when Joseph Swaine refused to allow
revenue officer George England onto his boat for fear of
damage to his nets. England shot him dead. The officer
was put on trial for murder and sentenced to death but was
later given a reprieve, causing the fishermen of Hastings to
go on strike in protest.

The Revenue were suspicious of the fishermen because
a common tactic was for a larger boat to come in with kegs

tied beneath the keel, which would be cut loose with weights attached to float just beneath the water – a practice known as 'sowing'. A cork float, identical to the kind used for crab or lobster pots, was used to mark the spot, and over the next few days local fishermen would come and collect the kegs a few at a time, 'creeping' them up with special hooks and concealing them under their nets or beneath the day's catch.

A lady visitor to Poole supposedly got an unexpected demonstration of the scheme as she was arriving into port by boat. She spotted the corks bobbing in the water and asked the captain what they were. When he told her that they were for lobster pots she took a fancy to see one, as she'd never seen how lobsters were caught before. The captain obliged and went to pull one up, only to reveal a pair of kegs instead of a pot. Unfortunately one of her fellow passengers was a local customs officer, and he had the captain return the kegs to the water, keeping a careful note of the exact spot they went down. The next day he kept a close eye on the local fishermen and soon spotted one hauling something in at the spot where he had left the kegs. The fisherman was arrested as soon as he set foot on dry land.

Despite the smuggler's best efforts to anchor the kegs firmly to the seabed, the rafts could sometimes come adrift. A trading vessel from Sunderland found sixty-two kegs floating off Newhaven in 1820. The captain did his legal duty and handed sixty-one kegs in to the customs office, but claimed that the last keg had broken while they were pulling it aboard. He blamed the merry behaviour of his crew on their excitement at reaching dry land after so long at sea.

At least one keg shared between a whole crew couldn't do too much damage, unlike an incident near Shoreham. The customs officers had made a huge seizure – over 400 kegs – and needed the help of the local troops to carry them all away. Two soldiers managed to save one of the kegs for themselves, sure that it wouldn't be missed out of so many, and tried to drink the whole thing in a single night. One of the men was due to be married the next day, but he never made it to his wedding: he was found lying dead on the beach the next morning and his friend was found nearby, unconscious, but luckily still alive.

If you've ever survived your own overindulgence, but found yourself wishing you hadn't, you may have needed a restorative. The hard-drinking men of Oxford University, who consumed plenty of smuggled cargo rather than go without brandy in the war years, had just the thing for you. While it's not listed specifically as a hangover cure, it is the only 'restorative' in a book otherwise devoted to alcoholic indulgences, so it doesn't seem likely that it's purely intended for treating the flu. The recipe makes enough for a whole hung-over party, but you can divide everything by six for a more sensible measure. Although it does contain gelatine, the punch should still be liquid: the calves-feet jelly was added for its nutritional qualities and to give the drink a silky feel, not to make it set.

RESTORATIVE PUNCH: THE ORIGINAL

Extract the juice from the peeling of one Seville orange and one lemon; the juice of six Seville oranges and six lemons, six glasses of calves-feet jelly in a liquid state, a sufficient quantity of loaf sugar (about half a pound); put the whole into a jug, pour on it one quart of boiling water; add four glasses of brandy, stir it well together, and it is fit for use.

R. *Cook,* Oxford Night Caps: A Collection of Receipts for Making Various Beverages *(1827)*

THE ALCHEMIST'S VERSION

9 leaves gelatine

100g sugar

6 oranges (Seville if you can get them)

6 lemons

500ml brandy

First, break the gelatine leaves into quarters and put them in the bottom of a small, heatproof bowl. Add just enough cold water to cover them, and leave the gelatine to soften. Meanwhile, put the sugar into a pan with the zest of one orange and one lemon, add 100ml of water and gently heat until the sugar has dissolved. Leave aside to cool. Next, take your softened gelatine and heat the bowl over a pan of boiling water until the gelatine has dissolved.

Strain the sugar syrup into a large heatproof jug or punchbowl.
Add the juice of the oranges and lemon, followed by the dissolved
gelatine. Finally, add 800ml of boiling water, then pour in the
brandy and stir.

Serve to your groaning party of hung-over university students to
get them back on their feet in no time.

Kegs were sometimes concealed in fresh water as well as salt, with local ponds and streams making good temporary storage spots. The inhabitants of Wiltshire acquired their nickname from an incident with the local Revenue while they were trying to retrieve some tubs from a pond at Bishops Canning. When the Revenue came unexpectedly on them with their hooks in the pond, the smugglers feigned stupidity. The officer asked them what they were doing and they pointed at the reflection of the moon, explaining that they were trying to get the big cheese out of the water. They flailed uselessly at the reflection with their rakes, wailing, until the officer gave up on them and left. The people of Wiltshire have been proud to call themselves the Moonrakers ever since.

Play-acting comes into a number of stories told about smugglers, especially in tales where they outwit the Revenue. One anecdote about the Mother Redcap pub in Wallasey has the customs officer drinking there when the smugglers were hoping to extract some casks from a hiding place in the building. To draw him away, one of the gang crept down to the shoreline and lay fully clothed at the edge of the water. Then the cry went up, 'A body down on the beach!' and the officer ran down to investigate, along with much of the rest of the pub. The locals encouraged him to check the drowned man's pockets, since he was 'in authority', and it was only as he was removing a watch that the dead man jumped up and hit him in the face. He got away with the assault as he claimed that he'd had a fit while walking on the sand and passed out. When he came to and discovered someone rifling through his pockets, he had naturally reacted to defend himself from the thief.

Before the blockade, 'derricking' had been a popular way of getting contraband off small boats unnoticed: boats would sail up to a cliff side, and a group waiting at the top would haul their cargo up with ropes and a pulley. The procedure wasn't without its dangers: a group of smugglers near Branscombe tried to use a farm gate as a platform to hold the cargo, but found that someone needed to go up on the gate with the cargo to stop it falling off. When they attempted the run in a high wind, the young man on the gate was dashed against the cliff and killed. In general, though, it had been a good technique in the days when there weren't many officers, since they tended to concentrate their attention on the beaches where they knew ships could land. But with the establishment of the blockade, every clifftop was watched, leaving no safe place for derricking.

One group near Beachy Head found a clever way around the problem. At the spot where the smugglers set up their plan there was a beach that was wide enough for the blockade men to patrol at low tide; but at high tide the beach was completely submerged, and they had to patrol the top of the tall chalk cliffs instead. The smugglers disguised themselves as shepherds and, under the cover of collecting seabirds' eggs from the ledges of the cliff, enlarged a nook behind one ledge until it was large enough to hold two men and a number of kegs. Once it was finished they could climb up in the evening and hide themselves on the ledge, waiting for nightfall and for the high tide. Once the water had risen and driven the blockade men up to the top of the cliff, a boat would pull up under cover of darkness and the 'shepherds' would winch the kegs up to the ledge. Then they had another long wait for the tide to go out again and the blockade men to return to the beach, before some others from their crew could come and winch the kegs the rest of the way up. They managed this trick for quite some time before being betrayed by one of their accomplices. When the nook was discovered by the authorities, it had been made so large that they found fifty-six small kegs inside.

Although smugglers everywhere hoped that the government would eventually lose interest – as it so often did in such projects – the end of the blockade never came. In 1831, it was simply absorbed into the service that had been set up ten years earlier to cover the rest of the coast: the coastguard. The coastguard would evolve to become mainly a life-saving force and a naval reserve; even today, though, it also keeps a weather eye out for smugglers.

However, it was the reform of customs duties in 1850 that really did for spirit smuggling. The new levels of duty made the rewards too low compared to the risks. Besides, there was a new commodity to smuggle that was even higher in value per pound: opium. The era of drug-smuggling was beginning. It was an easy option: drugs were small in volume but high in value, and there was no need to integrate them back into the legal supply. However, they also changed the nature of smuggling by breaking the link with the wider community; unlike spirits, drugs were not a staple that most people would be willing to help bring in. The shift to drugs as a cargo changed the nature of smuggling from everyday resistance to organised crime, and also moved it well out of the scope of this book.

CHAPTER SIX

WE'LL DRINK AGAIN

The production of illicit spirits was a dying art by the start of the twentieth century. Increased enforcement was part of the story but wider changes in our attitude to food and drink as a nation also played an important part. In the later part of the nineteenth century, increasing interest from both the press and the government in public health, combined with the development of technology to detect problems in food and drink, led to a series of food adulteration scandals.

There were lead and mercury compounds found in sweets; rag pulp and horse-bone oil in butter; plaster of Paris in bread; iron filings and sand in tea; and beer was so routinely 'improved' that there were Beer Doctors who would come to your inn, diagnose the problem with your bad beer and give you some mysterious powders to pep it right back up. Even the adulterants had adulterants: you might think that it was safe to put some fire back into watered-down gin with a touch of cayenne pepper, not knowing that the pepper had already been adulterated with brick dust and red lead.

So when, in 1872, the *North British Daily Mail* published the results of their analysis of whisky samples from fifteen Glasgow public houses, it wouldn't have come as a shock if some of them had been a little bit doctored. But when it was revealed that all of them were so badly contaminated with methanol, fusel oil, turpentine and sulphuric acid that they were barely recognisable as whisky, there was an outcry. In response, whisky distillers and larger blenders began changing the way that they sold and marketed their whisky. Advertisements began emphasising that a particular brand was safe and pure. Producers stopped the traditional practice of selling their whisky to pubs by the barrel and trusting them to put it on tap; instead everything began to come out of the distilleries bottled, sealed and branded.

For the first time, the government also began requiring that local councils employ a public analyst to check the safety of food and drink sold in their borough, the precursor to modern food safety teams. The combination of regular enforcement and the need for brands to build trust began to take effect. At the start of the nineteenth century, you were no safer buying a legal drink than an illegal one, in fact you might be safer with the illegal one, but by the dawn of the twentieth century, when you bought a bottle of Haig, Dewar or Bells you could be fairly sure of getting safe, pure whisky. Something would have to cause a serious problem with the supply of safe legal spirits to have people willing to turn back to the uncertainties of the unmarked bottle. Unfortunately something very big was coming; not just one world war but two.

When war was declared on 3 September 1939, the population had none of the illusions that had accompanied the declaration of the First World War in 1914. This war would not be over by Christmas, starvation was a distinct possibility and strict government controls would be in place from the beginning. The Emergency Powers Bill had been passed in August, before the war had even begun; it allowed all current laws to be set aside in favour of 'defence regulations' that could be issued and amended by cabinet ministers and their departments at will. Boards and ministries were formed to regulate different areas of life; these included the Board of Trade, the Ministry of Food and the Ministry of Supply. Identity cards were issued immediately to every citizen – the first time mandatory papers had ever been used in Britain – and ration books soon followed.

Breaking a defence regulation was a strict liability offence, a crime where intent was irrelevant. Failure to know or understand all of the complex regulations was no defence. The burden of proof was also reduced, with the government able to detain anyone if it merely 'appeared expedient'. This new level of control over every aspect of daily life should have sounded the death knell for the black market and illegal trade. That was certainly the plan – but like so many plans, it failed to survive contact with reality. The black market deepened and broadened, taking in many who would have previously considered themselves upstanding, law-abiding citizens. When just a little extra butter is illegal, or a new suit more than once a year, then it is easy to become a criminal.

The existing underworld also found a new source of recruits: dodgers and deserters. Conscription was introduced for all men between the ages of eighteen and forty-one on the day that war broke out, with exceptions only for the medically unfit and those working in reserved occupations. Unsurprisingly, not all of those eligible were keen to go to war, and there was suddenly a lively market in doctors who would certify you unfit, officials who would lose your documents and employers who could claim you worked in a reserved occupation. There was even a market in men who had already been declared unfit, who would impersonate you in front of the medical board. Jack Brack was called up in 1939, but certified unfit due to an enlarged heart – and then, for almost a year, he was the heart of a small enterprise of impersonations. He attended medical boards in the place of others in at least eight boroughs, commanding fees of up to £200 a time, until he was caught.

For those who were unable to acquire legal-looking documentation, the only remaining alternative to joining up was to go on the run. Once they had officially failed to show up for training, they were classified as deserters.

Dodger and deserter alike relied upon the black market, where they could buy the forged identity cards and forged or stolen ration books that they needed in order to eat and walk around. With no access to a legal income, unless they had massive savings and a hideout or relatives who could conceal and support them, men on the run would often find that becoming black-marketeers or thieves themselves was the only way to make a living for the remainder of the war.

There was one last, desperate method to escape service. The army would usually reject convicted criminals, at least if they had proved poor soldiers. When brothers Brian and Patrick Williams, a soldier and a sailor, walked into the police station in Brighton and confessed to a string of robberies that had taken place a full three years earlier, the police had no choice but to reluctantly put them on trial. Brian got the result he wanted: the army didn't want him back, and he went to Borstal for three months before returning to civilian life. But Patrick had been a better sailor than his brother was a soldier, and the navy decided to keep him despite his crimes.

As for the spirits: well, when almost everything is part of the black market (stockings, chickens, furniture, butter, cigarettes, cosmetics, tinned fruit, car tyres, clothing, toys, sweets, coupons and even entire identities), separating out just one category becomes a difficult task. For everyone involved – from corner shops putting a little something aside for a favourite customer, to large gangs of professional criminals – spirits were just another item of inventory. They often weren't even the most profitable. Billy Hill, the leader of a criminal gang from Kentish Town, ex-jewel thief and by the early 1940s a major London racketeer, sold whisky by the barrel to pubs, but found that he could get more money selling sausage-skins to butchers because the shortage of those was so severe.

Spirits were technically still legally available, and not even rationed; but like many other luxuries, they were rationed by supply. Cocktails in their modern form had arrived in Britain from the USA in the 1920s with bartenders who were fleeing Prohibition, and the trend had become popular. However, if spirits were in short supply, the myriad other ingredients needed for complex cocktails were even more difficult to obtain. As a result, it was the simpler cocktails that became popular in the war years. Pink gin, requiring nothing more than gin and a bottle of bitters (one of which might last you the whole war), was a particularly popular choice.

PINK GIN COCKTAIL: THE ORIGINAL

1 dash Angostura bitters

2 oz gin

Shake well and strain into cocktail glass
Harry Craddock, from The Savoy Cocktail Book *(1930)*

THE ALCHEMIST'S VERSION

2 dashes bitters of your choice
50ml gin (ideally you want a Plymouth gin, not a London
dry, because this is an old navy recipe. On the other hand,
there's a war on! So use whatever you can get)

Drop the bitters into a Martini glass and swirl them around to
coat the inside. Some people pour out the excess, depending on
taste. It seems like a waste to do this in wartime, but you can do
so if you prefer. You could also make the most of your bitters by
tipping the excess into another glass to start on the next pink gin
— that seems to be in the best thrifty wartime spirit. Shake the gin
over ice and pour into your prepared glass.

Drink after a long shift operating the radar with the Women's
Auxiliary Air Force or building bombs in a munitions factory,
while chatting with other newly liberated working women. Refuse
to allow the neighbourhood gossips to be scandalised by you
drinking in public. They don't get to judge you until they learn to
operate radar equipment and spend the night saving lives.

The Scottish whisky industry had been in hard times since
the start of the 1900s. The government had been in the
grip of temperance fervour, increasing duty regularly and
steeply since the People's Budget of 1909. When munitions

production targets were missed in 1915 the Chancellor of the Exchequer, Lloyd George, blamed the problem on drink rather than the obvious lack of equipment and man-power. Luckily he didn't get the controls he wanted at that time and had to settle instead for passing the Immature Spirits Act, which required all whisky to be warehoused for a minimum of three years before sale. The long ageing process that Scottish whisky undergoes is now the pride of the industry, and ageing had been increasingly popular among the makers of good single malts for many years; but for the makers of cheap blends, the regulation was a great blow.

Things got progressively worse after Lloyd George was appointed Minister of Munitions, and 1917 was a sad year for the industry. All distilling in traditional pot stills was prohibited to conserve supplies of grain for food, and only the eight patent stills that produced industrial alcohol for military use were left running. There was still plenty of mature whisky in stores, but the release of that was also brought under tighter control. Traditionally, most whisky had been sold at between 52 and 59 per cent abv, but in February it became compulsory to sell whisky at no more than 40 per cent abv – a strength that has stuck for all but a few specialist cask-strength whiskies ever since. In munitions production areas, which covered most urban centres in the country, the maximum strength was a desultory 28.6 per cent abv. In April the release of stocks was also restricted, and the industry was not allowed to sell more than 50 per cent of the number of bottles sold before the war.

In 1918, the final year of the war, the duty on spirits was almost doubled and for the first time a maximum price per bottle of 9s was introduced, to prevent the industry passing on the full duty increase to the consumer. After the war ended, the ban on distilling was lifted, but the fixed price and restrictions on release remained – and when America voted in Prohibition in 1920, the industry was in real trouble. There were so many closures in the period before 1934, when the economy finally started to recover, that the number of operating distilleries had dropped to almost half those running at the start of the century. The losses might have been even worse if it had not been for a coordinated effort by the Distillers Company Limited and other large companies under the direction of the Scotch Whisky Association to buy up failing distilleries and to keep open, or safely mothball, as many of them as possible.

The industry and the economy were only just starting to recover when war broke out all over again. The fixed prices and controls on domestic release returned, but initially production was actually encouraged for export. The government needed large amounts of dollar currency to fund the purchase of weapons, food and equipment. Whisky was one of the best dollar earners now that Prohibition had ended, so large amounts of whisky flowed out of stills and barrels, but most of it was shipped away and little made it into the shops at home – at least, not legitimately.

When a little whisky did make it to the shops, a lot of it would immediately be squirrelled away by the proprietors to use in their questionably legal grey-market dealings with other shopkeepers. For everyone else, queuing was the only chance to have a shot at a little of these rare luxuries legally. If you saw a queue at any shop, it was a good indicator of something worth having; people would often join any queue they saw, only finding out what it was for and whether they could afford it when they reached the front. You'd have to be very lucky to join the right queue at the right time on the right day and buy yourself a real bottle at the fixed price of 13s 9d.

Perhaps, at the end of that queue, you would instead find yourself with two or three precious lemons or oranges, cocktail staples that were also in short supply. The Ministry of Food published a lot of leaflets with handy recipes to get around these shortages. The recipe they distributed for carrot marmalade was one of the most infamous and least successful, except as a source of entertaining anecdotes about how terrible it was. It turns out that just being the same colour isn't enough to make one food a good substitute for another. Using a little orange stretched out with more apple makes a much more pleasing condiment, even if it's not exactly what we know as marmalade. It can even be used to make an acceptable marmalade cocktail.

THE ORIGINALS

Carrot marmalade:
1 lb. Carrots; 4 Lemons (6, if small); 4lb Sugar; 7 tumblers Water.

Grate carrots and lemon rind. Squeeze lemon juice, and add water. Boil all together for ¾ hour. Then add sugar, and boil for a further 20 to 30 minutes, or until set.

Ambrose Heath, Two Hundred War-Time Recipes – From the Kitchen Front (1941)

Orange skin and apple marmalade:
3 Oranges (peel only); 3 Apples (may be windfalls); 1 lemon; 2½ lbs Sugar.

Cut the orange and lemon peel into slices, and peel and core the apples and slice them too. Soak all for 24 hours in 2½ pints of water or possibly 3 pints. Boil for about 1 to 1½ hours or until the skins are soft.

Ambrose Heath, Two Hundred War-Time Recipes (1941)

Marmalade cocktail: (6 people)
2 dessertspoonfuls Orange Marmalade
Juice of 1 big or 2 small Lemons
8 oz Gin

Shake carefully and pour out, squeezing a piece of orange rind into each glass

Harry Craddock, from The Savoy Cocktail Book (1930)

THE ALCHEMIST'S VERSIONS

For the cocktail:

½ lemon

*1 tsp marmalade (try making the carrot marmalade if you
want to be authentically disgusted, the orange and apple if you
want to be authentic but not completely ruin your gin; or use
shop-bought if you just want a cocktail and not a history lesson)*

50ml gin

*Shake all the ingredients over ice and strain into a Martini glass,
or whatever you have to hand. Garnish with a disc of carrot, slit
to the middle and pushed onto the rim of the glass.*

*Drink while imagining that the carrot is orange. You'll have to
imagine quite hard.*

For carrot marmalade:

110g carrots

350ml water

1 lemon

440g sugar

*Peel and grate the carrots then add to a large pan along with the
water and the juice and zest of the lemon. Bring to the boil, then
simmer for 45 minutes with the lid on. Add the sugar and heat
gently till dissolved, then bring back to the boil. Keep at a rolling
boil until the mixture measures 104 °C on a jam thermometer,
or until a teaspoon dropped onto a cold saucer begins to set — or*

just until you get bored and fed up, since it was notoriously
difficult to get this recipe to set properly. Take off the heat and
allow to cool a little, then put the 'marmalade' into a jar which
has been sterilized by heating in a 140°C oven for ten minutes.

For orange and apple marmalade:
1 large orange (peel only)
1 large apple, peeled, cored and chopped (preferably
a cooking apple like a Bramley)
1 lemon
400g sugar
500ml water

Cut the orange peel into long, thin strips and place in a large
pan with the apples and the zest and juice of half the lemon.
Add the water, cover and leave to soak for 24 hours, or at least
overnight. The next day, add the sugar and then bring the pan to
the boil. Simmer gently, uncovered, for around an hour until the
orange skins have become soft and slightly transparent. Bottle as
for carrot marmalade.

Elizabeth Moore in Bethnal Green was one of those shopkeepers who would receive some of the precious legal supply
of whisky. She ran a small off-licence with her husband
Stephen, and when a shipment came in, some would be
put aside immediately to be traded for some of her own

small luxuries and necessities to feed her family. One bottle would go to the butcher in exchange for a joint of meat, one to her son's teacher swapped for tea and another to a friend of her eldest son, who worked in a fishmonger and would put some fresh fish aside for her. This was all just part of the tight-knit community network that kept working-class areas alive through the shortages.

For those who didn't have friends in the right places but did have a bit of spare cash, there was the black market. The *Daily Mail* ran an exposé in 1944 entitled 'Welcome to Racket Town', in which their reporter bought a bottle of whisky in an alleyway in the anonymous town for £5 – more than five times the legal fixed price. Another paper revealed the town to be Leeds, but the practice was common everywhere. As well as costing a lot more, buying on the black market carried the risk that you might not get an authentic product. You just paid your money and you took your chances. In Glasgow in particular, there was a roaring trade in counterfeit whisky. Being close to the industry gave the counterfeiters access to small amounts of whisky as well as larger quantities of the empty bottles and labels needed to pull off a scam. At the same time, the large number of American and Canadian troops passing through the city gave them a ready and gullible market.

In Glasgow Central train station, it became common to see boys selling famous brands of whisky to troops who were shipping out at £5 a bottle. By the time the soldiers discovered that they'd been sold a bottle full of cold tea they were already on the train and travelling hundreds of miles away. At least the tea was safe to drink; elsewhere in Glasgow, publicans were snapping up barrels of whisky that had been watered down and then 'livelied' back up with the addition of meths and some burnt caramel for colouring. The publicans would have seen enough whisky in their time to know the stuff wasn't right, but they would keep coming back for more; a reputation for always having whisky in stock was good for custom, even if the whisky was potentially dangerous.

In London things were a little better, at least when the police weren't ruining the party. In January 1942, Benjamin Bennett was caught running a still in the scullery of his café on Asylum Road, Peckham. In the absence of sugar or grain, he was using the by-products from a sugar beet plant to make his wash. Flavouring essences to make his spirit taste like rum, whisky, gin and various liqueurs were found, and at the time of the raid he had just finished bottling three and a half gallons of cherry brandy. The still was a clean and efficient modern design and when the spirits were tested they were found to be just as good, if not better, than the spirits produced by commercial distilleries. The same had been true of the spirits produced by a Camberwell motor dealer who had been caught using a similar still and shut down two years earlier.

Stolen surgical spirit or industrial alcohol was another relatively safe, although not too pleasant, base for some bootleg spirits. Donald Hulme was regularly seen around

West End nightclubs selling bottles of Finlinson's Old English Gin, which he manufactured himself from surgical spirit and flavourings – at least until he was convicted as an accessory to a murder that he had probably in fact committed. He gained some notoriety at the time – even more so when he committed a second murder just after his release.

In Soho, Customs and Excise uncovered a major ring of bootleggers centred on the Granville Club in Albemarle Street. Six men and two women were arrested and convicted for stealing drums of industrial alcohol from a warehouse in Hammersmith and using them to make counterfeit spirits. They would colour, flavour and bottle them before applying labels from top brands, which were produced on the same presses used to print identity cards and ration books for deserters. They had been offering the public up to 2s 6d for empty bottles to fill with their wares and selling them in their own club as well as to others. A salesman would take a sample bottle of the real stuff to impress potential clients, before delivering pure hooch.

By 1942 the hooch problem had become a significant concern for the Air Ministry, whose pilots could be out partying on leave one night then in the skies over Germany the next, and so were more at risk than other branches of the military. They ordered samples of captured hooch to be analysed and found that in general, the quality was even worse than that seen in America during Prohibition – not really surprising when you consider that America's shores and other borders had been notoriously leaky, whereas the British shores were patrolled by fully armed enemy U-boats.

The other services eventually caught up with the concerns of the Air Ministry after a series of disturbing incidents. In March, a Canadian airman went berserk at a London hotel and attacked several other guests before enough guards arrived to hold him down. In a separate incident at a canteen in Waterloo, an able seaman fell asleep at his table and had to be roused by the manager-ess. When he was woken the sailor started fighting with her and one or two others who tried to intervene, before diving head first through a high window. Both incidents were blamed on brain damage caused by methyl alcohol poisoning, although neither was fatal. Later, in May, eleven men and three women died in a single episode in Glasgow, and four company directors were paralysed after just one small whisky and soda at a London hotel. The directors were personal friends of Colonel Charles Kerr, Baron of Teviot, who was furious enough to bring the matter up in a debate in the House of Lords. Due to these and a rash of other similar incidents, a special detachment of medical officers was formed under the Provost Marshal's depart-ment to investigate.

If top hotels were willing to purchase whisky on the black market (and the accidental paralysis of four company directors surely shows that they were), then they must have been equally desperate to track down other elusive cocktail ingredients for their demanding customers. Bartender Harry Craddock had popularised the dry Martini at the Savoy just prior to the war, and dry vermouth was essential to that and many other contemporary cocktails. No records of how they solved the problem survive; but over on the island of Jersey, which was under Nazi occupation at that time, an enterprising doctor created his own substitute to go with his homemade gin and recorded the recipe in his memoir.

WARTIME DRY MARTINI: THE ORIGINAL

My next problem was to find a substitute for dry Martini. I already had a small barrel of sweet Martini which had been given to me by an Italian, but none of us fancied it at the time and I was confident that I could make something with more customer appeal. Before the end most of them had to take the sweet Martini and like it, but this was fairly early on, and my friends more choosy than they became later.

I got hold of a demijohn of dry Jersey cider and divided it up into bottles. In the first I put a teaspoonful each of Tincture of Quinine and Tincture of Gentian, with half a bay leaf, and left it for three days. This proved to be too dry and too redolent of bay, so the dose of quinine and of bay were both halved and marinated as before.

*After straining through an old piece of fine linen, I had a
very good imitation of dry Martini which met with universal
approval, although some of my friends took it with a dash of the
despised sweet Martini in addition.*

Dr John Lewis, A Doctor's Occupation *(1982)*

THE ALCHEMIST'S VERSION

1 tbsp tonic syrup or concentrate
½ tsp Angostura bitters
¼ bay leaf
500ml dry cider

*Since tinctures of gentian and quinine are less than common
these days, it seems truer to the spirit of this emergency vermouth
substitute to use ingredients you are more likely to have lying
around. Angostura or any other classic-style bitters contain
a fair amount of gentian (at least as far as anyone can work
out, given their recipe is a well-kept secret), and the syrup or
concentrate you can buy for making your own tonic water is the
most concentrated source of quinine you are likely to get hold of.*

*Use an empty bottle, a little larger than the cider bottle — an old
vermouth bottle is, unsurprisingly, ideal — and add the tonic
syrup, bitters and bay. Pour in the cider, seal the bottle and leave
for three days. When your Cider Vermouth is ready, strain out
the bay through a cheesecloth or tea strainer, then return the
liquid to the bottle.*

Enjoy mixed into a dry Martini with friends, but be sure that they leave for home before the start of curfew.

The 'hooch madness' defence became a popular one for officers who were late returning from leave, got into fights or were arrested for being drunk and disorderly. However, the courts would only accept the plea if they gave up their supplier, so many suppliers were easily caught. Many hooch suppliers claimed that they were merely producing the spirit under the instructions of a bigger criminal who they could not identify, but no definite evidence of a shadowy Mr Big of the hooch racket was ever found. He may simply have been a tall tale told in the hopes of getting a reduced sentence. Certainly very little dent was made in the hooch problem; new suppliers would pop up as soon as the old ones were shut down. Some American bases became so concerned about the problem that they would issue a free bottle of real whisky or gin from stores to any man going on leave, in the hopes that it would keep him off the hooch.

As for the real stuff, a loophole meant that mature whisky from the warehouses of distilleries that went bankrupt could be sold at auction outside the quota system and above the fixed maximum price. When a large batch of eight-year-old blended whisky went up for auction in Belfast in 1944, the agents of a London nightclub snapped it up at £28 7s 6d a gallon, or around £4 7s a bottle, even though the fixed price by that time was only £1 5s 9d. Some city traders saw easy money to be made in the unsellable stocks of valuable mature whisky that struggling small distilleries had in their warehouses. They would buy up a controlling interest in a company and then sell off the stocks of whisky in a series of complex transactions designed to evade both the quota system and the excess profits tax, which was set at a high level designed to prevent war profiteering. Once the warehouses were empty they would dump their stocks in the now valueless company, which would usually go quickly bankrupt. A number of unique distilleries were lost forever in this way, but some were saved when members of the Whisky Association bought them up, seeing potential even without their lost stocks, and continuing their stewardship of the industry as a whole through the continuing hard times.

Production of gin, on the other hand, had been diverted almost entirely to the navy, where the daily tot was still an established practice that would survive until the 1970s. Although it was known as the rum ration, the daily measure could be dispensed in any spirit, and home-produced gin was a good choice at a time when shipping rum (or anything else) across the Atlantic was so hazardous due to the constant threat of U-boat attacks. Many surviving gin distilleries have close ties with the navy because of this supply. When the Blackfriars Distillery suffered a direct hit during the Plymouth Blitz, a telegram was sent to all ships to let them know that although the offices had been hit, the actual still room had survived intact. It gave the crews one bright spot in the otherwise terrible news about a maritime city with close ties to the navy.

Some rum was still making it across the ocean, despite the dangers, but all of it went straight to either the navy or the army, who had reintroduced a rum ration for front-line troops during the harsh winter of 1914–15. In the Second World War, the rum ration for the army was given only to troops living under sustained fire or about to go over the top; the latter received a double ration equivalent to around seven units of alcohol, enough for them to be going into battle really quite drunk. Spirits were also given as a first treatment for shock in battlefield triage, and were one of the perks for recovering soldiers in hospital. This egg flip recipe featured in a Second World War catering manual for battle units, in the section covering recommended diet for the sick or wounded.

EGG FLIP: THE ORIGINAL

Break 2 eggs, beat the white to a froth, then add the yolks and rebeat. Fold in a cupful of hot milk, add one teaspoonful of brandy, a little sugar and a pinch of nutmeg.

Extract from a logistics corps field manual (c. 1943)

THE ALCHEMIST'S VERSION

2 eggs

1 tsp caster sugar

A pinch of grated nutmeg

1 tbsp brandy or rum

150ml whole milk

Separate the eggs and beat the whites until they form soft peaks with an electric whisk. In a separate bowl, beat the yolks with the sugar and nutmeg until light and fluffy. Add the brandy or rum to the bottom of a large mug, then heat the milk, add it to the mug and stir well. Stir the yolk and sugar gently into the milk, then top with the whites.

Drink in a hospital bunk while wondering what has happened to the rest of your unit and hoping that you might be unwell enough to be sent home.

With so much of the good stuff in the possession of the army, a large amount of spirits as well as other stores and equipment were 'liberated' into the black market by corrupt stores officers or stolen in transit. Theft of stores from the navy, army and air force institutes, who organised canteens, shops and recreations for all three forces, became such a problem that they began shipping shoes with all the left shoes in one crate and all the right shoes in the other. Such tactics would pose a problem for opportunistic thieves who were grabbing a crate without being sure what they were getting, but would have been no deterrent to an inside man. At the Portsmouth navy barracks, a whole crew were in on the scheme to claim stores for unmanned crafts and rum rations for non-existent sailors to sell on to local publicans. They even stripped the mahogany furniture out of the wardrooms on the unmanned ships to sell on. Since nothing but ugly, regulation Utility Furniture had been produced for years, the stylish chairs and tables were incredibly popular on the black market.

Thefts weren't always so subtle, or even intended for the black market. On one particularly miserable voyage on a troop ship in August 1943, three assistant cooks decided that they'd had enough and smashed in the door to the storeroom with axes. They liberated food and drink including forty-four bottles of whisky and over 800 bottles of beer, handed them out to the troops and had a party. When the party was over, the culprits were tried in a civilian court in Liverpool. Perhaps they had been trying to get themselves out of the service and in this they succeeded, but they were lucky not to end up court-martialled on charges of mutiny.

The practice of stealing from workplaces was so widespread and so generally accepted as a lesser crime than 'real' theft that it had its own name: pilfering. The railways were a major source of pilfered goods, since large quantities of valuable and rationed items were transported by train and with most able-bodied men away at war, the security was poor. Railway workers also had a generally bad relationship with their management, pay was low and conditions were harsh. Most railway workers regarded a little something off the back of the train as a normal perk of the job and the slim chance of getting caught taking it as an occupational hazard. Attitudes on the docks were much the same. A sixty-year-old foreman cooper on a London wharf who was caught and convicted of stealing a bottle of rum said to the magistrate after he was sentenced that it was just 'one of those things that happen now and again', while a foreman at Paddington Station who was caught stealing damaged parcels told the court that no one had seemed interested in the parcels, and the temptation had just been too great.

The large import/export and manufacturing company Kearley & Tonge decided to hire in an extra guard just to deal with the pilfering problem at their Durward Street warehouse. By the time the CID raided his house he was found in possession of twenty-two bottles of gin, fifty bottles of whisky and another fifty of brandy, along with cigarettes, chocolates, soap, tinned foods, salt and cakes. Not only did convictions for large systemic thefts like this one fail to act as a deterrent to others, but many cases went to court that were clearly not worthy of prosecution. One of these was the case of Leonard Watson.

Leonard was the leader of the Heavy Rescue Squad.

The squad's job was to be first on the scene after a bombing and try to make the unstable ruins safe enough to go about the job of digging out survivors – or bodies. When they were done shoring up, they assisted the other rescuers with the search and recovery. It was a difficult, dangerous and traumatic job, so after the squad had finished digging the survivors out of the ruins of a bombed pub, Watson had thought nothing of picking up a quarter-full bottle of gin that had somehow survived the bombing intact to hand around to his men as a pick-me-up. He was tried for looting – and convicted, since as an honest man he felt he had to plead guilty to taking the bottle, even though few reasonable people would view it as looting.

The council officers whose job it was to report these incidents attracted great hatred. Even worse were those assigned to go out and try to actively persuade shopkeepers and publicans to break the law. In Hove, three plainclothes police officers decided to get close to the two female owners of the See-Saw Club, Margery Moss and Elizabeth Morgan, to learn whether they were serving drinks after hours. One of the officers posed as an RAF pilot and charmed the pair, inviting them out for dinner. After the men had paid for dinner and escorted them home, Moss and Morgan politely invited them in for a drink. Even though it was a friendly offer to a date, not a commercial transaction, the two were still convicted of serving after hours. They were fined a total of £250 between them – and worse, the club lost its licence, putting them out of business.

At least Moss and Morgan had the remains of their stock to console them. It wasn't just alcoholic drinks that were in short supply: production had stopped of most fizzy drinks and cordials too, leading to a terrible shortage of mixers for long drinks. Creativity and substitution came into their own here as well. No lime cordial to make a gimlet? Try a teaspoonful of lime curd! None of that either? Luckily the Ministry of Food were offering a recipe that made the best of a limited supply of citrus and egg to make an economy curd.

THE ORIGINALS

Gimlet:

½ Gin

½ Lime Juice Cordial

Use Old-Fashioned glass, stir, add ice, and serve
Harry Craddock, *from* The Savoy Cocktail Book *(1930)*

Lemon Curd:

1oz margarine; 1 level tablespoonful cornflour; 1 lemon
(2, if small); ¼ pint water; 5oz granulated sugar; 1 egg

Peel the rind off the lemons, put into the water and bring to the
boil. Beat the egg and cornflour, add the lemon juice and strain
the boiling water over. Return to the pan, add the sugar and stir

over heat 3 mins. Add the margarine and stir it in well, bottle immediately.

Ministry of Food advisory (1943)

THE ALCHEMIST'S VERSIONS

For the gimlet:
2 tsp lime curd (you can make the wartime
curd below, or use shop-bought)
25ml water
50ml gin

Spoon the lime curd into the bottom of a short tumbler and add the water slowly, stirring well as you do. Add the gin and give it another good stir, then add ice and serve. It's not quite the same as it was before the war, but it's not too bad.

For the lime curd:
Zest and juice of 2 limes
150ml water
1 egg
1 tbsp cornflour
150g sugar
30g margarine

Put the lime zest and water into a large pan and bring to the boil. While it is coming to the boil, beat the egg and sprinkle over the cornflour a little at a time, stirring continuously to prevent lumps. Then add the juice of both limes, a little at a time. Once the water has boiled, pass it through a sieve into a jug, then immediately add it to the egg while stirring. Transfer everything back to the pan and add the sugar. Heat gently until the sugar has dissolved, then bring back to the boil and simmer for 3 mins. Mix in the margarine and then bottle as for carrot marmalade (see page 188), or simply pour into a small bowl for immediate use.

Technically, for authenticity, your margarine should be made of whale oil; but since this is both disgusting and now illegal, it is fine to stick with something based on vegetable oil.

Many women had been left running businesses, or at least looking after whatever remnants of a business the war had left them. Elizabeth Williamson had been hired as a secretary by the Laphroaig distillery in 1934 and had quickly gained the trust of the owner, impressing him with her efficiency and clear business acumen. Gradually she had been given more responsibility, and when war broke out and the company lost most of its male employees, Elizabeth was chosen to run the distillery – not just because she was the only one left to do it, but because she was the best-qualified person, men or no men. Unfortunately, because of its strategic location, the distillery had also been requested for use by the government, a request which could not be refused.

So Williamson was appointed government liaison, in addition to her other responsibilities.

Production was shut down, troops were billeted in some of the malt barns and the other barns were used for the storage of ammunition and high explosive shells. Williamson took charge of the inventory of munitions, signing off personally on deliveries to incoming warships. She also politely but firmly let the Ministry of Works know that while the malt barns were available for use, the grain lofts were essential to the operation of the accompanying farm. The Ministry withdrew their request to use them, a concession not many managers could have obtained. Even fewer could have managed to keep their warehouse manager safe from conscription by obtaining a hardship exemption for him, on the basis that his work looking after the extensive warehoused stock was 'urgent work of national importance'. It was Williamson's promise that if the whisky made it through the war it would bring in £3 million in duty for the beleaguered exchequer that sealed the deal, and that promise was most certainly true. Keeping those 8,000 casks safe from the more than 200 soldiers billeted on the premises was also a task at which few could have succeeded. Once Williamson's casks had been shepherded safely through the war she turned her hand to marketing, making Laphroaig into one of the world's most celebrated single malts – but that's another story.

While Elizabeth Williamson was tending her stock of real whisky that could not be sold, others were making promises to sell whisky that did not exist. John Firth was a manager at the NAAFI in Maida Vale, and also a seven-times-convicted felon, which only goes to show the depth of the labour shortage with so many away at war. In his position he could easily have stolen from the stores, but he thought that it would be easier and less risky to simply promise spirits from his stores to pubs and clubs, take the money in advance and then never return. His customers were convinced to part with their money by his NAAFI credentials, and in theory they should have been unable to report him, because that would mean admitting they had tried to buy from the black market. Unfortunately for Frith, he eventually encountered some customers who cared more about punishing him than about saving themselves. The owners of the Windmill Club in London and the Flowerpot Hotel in Macclesfield were the ones who came forward, having lost £240 between them; and the considerable distance between the two demonstrates just how widespread his scam had become before it was shut down. After seeing Frith sent to jail, the two proprietors were happy to accept their own small fines with good grace.

Although the war ended in 1945, the controls and rationing only grew stricter for the next few years. The economy had been devastated, and huge debts were owed to America. The production of goods for export to America was prioritised over goods for the home market, in order to close the so-called 'dollar gap'. The whisky industry benefited from this push to export, gaining special permission directly from Churchill to resume production in 1944 – before the war had even come to its official end. The consumer was not so lucky: under a new regulation, whisky producers were granted access to grain to restart production on the condition that they exported four out of every five cases they bottled. Behind the scenes, there were also shortages of aged whisky after the long years of war, and stocks needed to be built up. Even after the official controls were released, it wasn't until 1959 that the industry dropped its own unofficial rationing of stock.

With the war over but the shelves still empty, and conditions not noticeably improved, it's no wonder that the public was losing patience with rationing controls. Even those who had previously virtuously abstained started to buy from the ever-expanding black market. The neighbourhood 'spiv' became a figure of affection, standing on a box in the local market in his trilby hat and his loud suit with wide, padded shoulders. A spiv dispensed entertainment as well as whisky and nylons. They sold their produce by pitching, starting off by offering whatever they were selling at twice what it was worth, even on the black market, and then gradually reducing the price. Buy too soon, and you were getting ripped off; wait too long and you might miss out altogether. The technique generates a sense of tension and excitement that home shopping channels still exploit to make late-night sales.

The spiv had become such a well-loved figure that when two cartoonists from Exeter published a spoof magazine from the Spivs' Union, offering memberships for a shilling, it was an instant hit. By February 1949 the union had 1,300 members, including actor Dirk Bogarde, and the magazine was publishing issues quarterly. You could by a union badge or tie pin featuring the President of the Spivs' Union, Ivor Racket, and you could even take an annual trip to the seaside with the Hull Spivs' Club or watch a Spiv Panto. Streets rang with the sound of kids singing the Spivs' anthem, which had been published in the *Spivs' Gazette*, to the tune of the popular song 'Side By Side':

> *Oh, we've all made a barrel of money,*
> *Maybe you think that we're funny.*
> *As we travel along, singing a song,*
> *Side by side.*
> *It may be a little risky,*
> *Driving a lorry of whisky,*
> *But we travel the road, sharing our load,*
> *Side by side.*
> *We all have a racket.*
> *It may be big or small,*
> *But if we make a packet,*
> *It doesn't matter at all.*
> *Some people work for a living,*
> *But we much prefer to keep spivving,*
> *And we travel along, singing a song,*
> *Side by side.*

The stylish spiv needed a stylish drink, but one that could still be made with the limited resources at his disposal. Maybe something that wasn't quite what it seemed – like most of his merchandise. This faux-champagne cocktail is just perfect for the spiv who is all mouth and trousers.

CHAMPAGNE COCKTAIL: THE ORIGINAL

Put into a wine glass one lump of Sugar, and saturate it with Angostura Bitters. Having added to this 1 lump of Ice, fill the glass with Champagne, squeeze on top a piece of lemon peel, and serve with a slice of orange.

Harry Craddock, from The Savoy Cocktail Book *(1930)*

THE ALCHEMIST'S VERSION

Champagne cider cocktail:
Bitters of your choice (Angostura is traditional, but
orange goes particularly well if you have it)
150ml dry cider, chilled
1 lemon
1 orange

Put four drops, or a good dash, of bitters into the bottom of a champagne flute (sugar isn't necessary with the added sweetness of the cider), then pour in the cider. Cut a big disc of zest from

the lemon, at least an inch across, and squeeze it over the drink.
Finally, cut a slice from the middle of the orange, cut that into
quarters and then slit one wedge up the middle before sliding
it onto the rim of the glass. What a fancy figure you'll cut with
this. Just be sure to hide the bottle and then absolutely refuse to
admit to anyone that you are not drinking champagne. This is
champagne, it is. Why is it that people never believe you when
you tell them that?

As the economy slowly recovered and legal spirits began to
return to the shelves plentifully and at a reasonable price,
the spiv faded away. Only an echo of his memory remains
in popular culture, epitomised by cockney wide-boy characters like Del Boy of *Only Fools and Horses*. With the demise of
the spiv, the last significant episode of romantically illicit
drinking came to an end. The modern reality is, unfortunately, far from romantic.

CHAPTER SEVEN

A SCOTTISH FAIRY TALE

When the SS *Politician* ran aground just off the small
Hebridean island of Eriskay on the morning of
4 February 1941, her cargo would spark one of the
most enduring modern fairy tales. Down in her holds she
was carrying cars, bikes, cotton, soap, bed springs and
many other useful but pedestrian items. More importantly, in hold number five she was carrying 22,000 cases
of whisky.

During the war, whisky for consumption was in short
supply – but large quantities were sitting stored in casks,
slowly ageing, while their release onto the home market
was prohibited by wartime regulations. Some of these were
stored in areas that were under bombardment, putting
the highly flammable spirits in terrible danger. When the
Number 12 warehouse at the Banff distillery was strafed
by a lone German Junker, the casks stored there caught
alight, bursting and flying through the air, sending riv-
ers of blue fire flowing down the streets. The only way to

stop the spread of the blaze was to stave in the remaining casks, letting gallons of whisky pour out and soak away into the ground where it would only ever be appreciated by the local waterfowl (which were noticeably drunk for several days afterwards). The remaining stores had to be evacuated before they could come to any more harm.

A collection of some of the very best Scottish whisky was bottled, boxed and crated to send out for sale to the American 'millionaire's market'. The special bottlings were given rich names like King's Ransom, VVO Gold Bar, McCallum's Perfection, PD Special and Haig Royal. They came from the oldest, most valuable casks, and were bottled overproof, even though regulations forced whisky for sale at home to be diluted to 40 per cent abv before sale. Some of the whisky was packaged in large, elaborate decanters or loaded still in the cask onto a train bound for the docks at Liverpool – and, ultimately, hold number five of the SS *Politician*.

Had the whisky made it to the USA – where war was still, for a few more months at least, something happening to other people – it might have become part of a cocktail scene that was still recovering after the end of Prohibition in 1933. Bartenders who had fled to Europe during that time were fleeing back again to escape occupation or bombings. They brought with them, among other things, a taste for Scotch, and a few questionably Scottish but certainly delicious recipes.

A SCOTTISH FAIRY TALE

BOBBY BURNS COCKTAIL: THE ORIGINAL

½ Italian Vermouth
½ Scotch Whisky
3 dashes Benedictine

Shake well and strain into a cocktail glass. Squeeze lemon peel on top.

One of the very best Whisky Cocktails. A very fast mover on Saint Andrew's Day.

Harry Craddock, from The Savoy Cocktail Book *(1930)*

THE ALCHEMIST'S VERSION

25ml dry vermouth
25ml good single malt whisky
5ml (1 tsp) Benedictine
Twist of lemon zest

Add all the liquid ingredients to a cocktail shaker filled with ice, and shake well. Strain into a chilled Martini glass, and finish with a twist of lemon zest. Sip while doing your best American millionaire impression and pretending that the Politician never sank. No, not at all! It made it to you quite safely, and a good job too. This whisky is excellent.

The *Politician* was a fast steamship that had been built as the *London Merchant* in 1923, and she had been in trouble because of whisky once before. In 1924 she had been taking a cargo of whisky down to South America and on the way, made the mistake of stopping over in Portland, Oregon. There, with America still under Prohibition, the Oregon State Prohibition Director enthusiastically seized her cargo. The ship's captain refused to leave without it and notified the British Embassy, who complained to the authorities in the strongest of terms. It was established that the cargo had already been approved, passed and sealed by the federal authorities – so the Prohibition Director had clearly broken the seals of his superiors in order to seize it. He was swiftly corrected, and forced to write a grovelling apology for sparking an international incident with his misplaced zeal. The *London Merchant* was allowed to go on her way to South America without any further problems.

In 1935, the *London Merchant* was sold to the Charente Steamship Company. Then, following the outbreak of war, she was pressed into service running merchant shipping between Liverpool and the USA across the perilously U-boat-infested waters of the North Atlantic. However, it would not be the enemy that sank the renamed *Politician* in the end, but the treacherous waters of the Minch, a strait in north-west Scotland. Having loaded up with whisky and other goods at Liverpool, the *Politician* was headed up to Scotland to meet up with a convoy, rather than risk the Atlantic crossing alone. The route would normally have passed around the outside of the Outer Hebrides rather than risk the dangerous passage up between the islands and the mainland, but with U-boats waiting out in the Atlantic, it was thought that the unpredictable currents and tides of the Minch were the safer option.

A lot of wild theories have been posited about the cause of the shipwreck: perhaps the crew were drunk, or the bridge officer mistook the shallow Sound of Eriskay for the deeper Sound of Barra. Some have even suggested that the rocks near Eriskay might have contained enough magnetic lodestone to spin the ship's compass round the wrong way, or that the local residents willed the ship onto the rocks with their desire for the cargo. But the truth is that it's just a dangerous area, and notoriously difficult to navigate. Ships have been getting into difficulties in its waters for as long as they have been trying to pass through – but unlike the *Politician*, those ships weren't carrying a hold full of whisky.

When they ran aground on the rocks, the crew had no idea where they were. They broadcast a distress call stating incorrectly that they were south of Barra – more than twenty miles from their actual position – and as the storm worsened, the captain lowered a rowing boat to evacuate all non-essential personnel. A young boy on the Eriskay shore was watching, bemused; he could tell that the ship was in no danger, as it was solidly beached on the rocks of the strait. The rowing boat, on the other hand, was tossing wildly on the rough seas and in severe danger of being dashed to pieces against the cliffs. Luckily it did wash up safely on a beach, although its landing place was surrounded by unscaleable cliffs, leading the crew to conclude that they were stranded on an uninhabited island. They started gathering supplies, lighting fires and settling in, anticipating a long wait for rescue. Fortunately, a fishing vessel alerted by the young boy was already on its way to pick them up and on reaching them, it delivered them back to the *Politician* along with the correct information about their position.

When, after several hours of fruitless searching in the wrong area, the local lifeboat finally received the ship's actual position, the crew were taken off the ship for the night and over to Barra, where local families put them up. Having broken into hold number five while they waited, they took with them as many bottles of whisky as they could fit in their pockets, as gifts for their hosts and themselves. Word about the cargo quickly spread across the islands – but the islanders had to wait and see whether it would all be taken away by the salvors before they had a chance to get to it themselves.

It took five days for a salvage vessel to arrive, but during that time the ship's officers were on and off the *Politician* constantly, so no attempts were made on the cargo; besides, the islanders didn't want to steal the whisky while someone else still had a claim on it. The tradition had always been that anything washed up on the shores of the islands, or rescued from the nearby waters, was regarded as a gift to the islanders from the sea – Cuile Mhoire, bounty from the Virgin Mary's treasure chest. So if the salvors couldn't refloat the ship and abandoned it, then by their own laws, if not by the actual law, the cargo would be the islanders' to take.

The salvage vessel sent to the *Politician* was the *Ranger*. For over a month its crew worked at removing the cargo from the dry holds (mostly cars, cotton and bikes) as well as sending in divers to assess the condition of the ship and determine whether it could be refloated. The damage was extensive, and while four of the holds were dry or only leaking slightly, two others were completely tidal, meaning that the holes in them were so large that the water inside rose and fell with the tide as well as being covered with a slick of engine oil a foot thick. Those holds were number six and the all-important hold number five.

While it was important to the islanders – and would soon take on huge significance for the local revenue officer – the cargo in hold number five was, in the view of the salvage team, not worth saving. That was the official verdict, anyway, although it didn't stop the divers from acquiring a few cases for their own personal use. Over the course of the salvage operation the *Ranger* made several trips back to Glasgow with loads of salvaged cargo; on the first trip the boat was boarded by Customs, who found the stash of whisky in the forecastle and impounded it. On the second trip, the crew slung the whisky over the side of the ship in a bag when they entered the harbour and made arrangements for a smaller boat to collect it for them later, in much the same manner as the smugglers of a hundred years previously.

Still, a few personal drams aside, the whisky was officially being abandoned. The local customs officer, Charles McColl, had been concerned about the contents of hold five since he first learned that it might hold whisky – but he had not met with much cooperation from the salvage crew. Their job was to safely retrieve any cargo that still had value to the owners and insurers of the ship, not to concern themselves with any potential loss of excise by the Revenue. The whisky had been shipped with no duty paid because it was going out of the country, so although the retail price would have been well over £200,000, the actual value of the whisky to the owners was less than £50,000. Even that was only assuming that it had not been spoilt by the salt water and the oil – which much of it had. To them it simply wasn't worth the cost of removing it.

But from the Revenue's point of view, every bottle that made it into unofficial circulation was a loss of around 12s – and there were more than 250,000 bottles on that ship. They didn't even need them rescued, only kept from circulation; it didn't matter to the Revenue whether the whisky was salvaged, destroyed or sent to the bottom of the ocean. Still, without the cooperation of the salvors, there was little Charles McColl could do to achieve any of those ends.

After repeated requests, he was finally shown around the ship on 8 March. When he saw how much whisky there was, he asked for a watch to be mounted after the salvors left, but was told that it was too dangerous and too expensive. In any case, the only people to take the job would be islanders, and they would be no deterrent at all to their friends. McColl had the hatch closed and sealed it with the customs seal before he left, though he knew that this would be about as much protection as an umbrella in a hurricane. The salvors left on 12 March, leaving the *Politician* to the tender mercies of the islanders.

The next night was like an unofficial regatta. Boats and crews came from as far away as Mull, Harris, Lewis, Skye and even Gairloch on the mainland, all keen to try their hand at the already legendary whisky. Men were stopping on the deck of the *Politician* to cheerfully greet friends and relatives who they hadn't seen in years, brought together again by the great quest for drowned whisky.

Down in the hold, the going was tough. At high tide the water covered even the entrance to the hold; at low tide it was still more than half full, and with the thick layer of oil covering the surface swimming was impossible, let alone diving for the cases. A few different techniques were developed. Norman Macmillan would later boast of inventing the 'whisky spear', which he hammered by hand out of a boathook to create a pointed end like a halberd which he could push under the wire wrapping of a case before hooking it up out of the water. Others were content to simply hang from the rafters and bat about in the soup of oil and water with a long spar of wood until they could bring a crate to the surface, where it could be lifted up with a loop of cloth.

There was no shortage of cloth: a huge number of bales had been ruined by oil and water, and then left behind by the salvors. While they were no use any more for selling or making into clothes, they did make excellent slings for moving whisky. Similarly, the sacks from the ruined cargo of salt and china clay were ideal for storing loose bottles once their contents had been emptied out onto the decks.

Those decks were, thanks to the position of the ship on the rocks, tilting at a dangerously steep angle, and slick with oil. The clay and salt helped a little with grip, but the process of getting at the whisky was still a dangerous and sometimes hilariously slapstick one. If you were lucky enough to have found space for your fishing boat on the down side of the ship, then all you had to do was climb up out of the hold and slip and slide your way down the deck to the rail, then clamber along the rail and over other people's whisky piles until you found your own. Once the tide had filled the hold and put an end to the night's whisky fishing, you could lower the crates and bags of bottles down to your boat at your leisure. If you had been unlucky enough to arrive late and had to anchor your boat around by the up side of the deck, you would have to first clamber up to the rail and then haul your crates up the slippery slope of the deck in a sling of fabric before you could pass them down off the deck.

Despite the hard work and dangerous conditions, there was a festival atmosphere on the *Politician*. The hold was lit up like a mystical cave, with myriad lamps and candles on every surface – so many had been found on board that there was no need to ration them. Spontaneous sing-songs took place around the beautiful inlaid piano in the dining saloon – the local schoolmaster desperately wanted it for his school-room, but it just wasn't possible to fit it on any of the boats. Teenage crewmen took delight in sliding around the oily decks and causing mischief. Every now and then, one would call a false alarm of 'Police!', just to see everyone else slip and scramble for the boats until they realised that the police were nowhere in sight. The jokes were taken with surprisingly good humour, given the genuine danger of being caught.

Once you sailed back with your haul, the night was still not over: the crates needed hiding from the eyes of the excise, as well as from neighbours who weren't lucky enough to have access to a boat. The great grassy dunes that fill the space between the sea and the higher rocks of the Hebrides are geographically and ecologically unique – properly called the machair – and here was where most of the cases were immediately buried, with a tuft of gorse or a pile of rocks left to mark the spot. Leave a mark that was too obvious, and the chances were that someone else would take your stash; but leave one too subtle and although no one else would find it, a worse tragedy would happen: neither would you. The machair would keep your whisky forever, just as the bottom of the sea might have done if you hadn't rescued it.

'Rescuing' the whisky was exactly how the islanders saw their work in the dark, oily hold. Cases of good whisky simply could not be allowed to sink into the salty ocean, where they would never be tasted by anyone. It would be a crime and a tragedy not to attempt the retrieval. So while some were undoubtedly annoyed to find their stashes taken by people who hadn't been willing to brave the dangers of the waves themselves, others took it all as part of the fun and festival of the event. They saw themselves as having no more right to the cases than anyone else. The important thing was that the whisky was drunk, and not simply left to drown.

The small communities of the Hebrides may have been isolated from the mainland, but they were famous for producing good sailors. As a result, many local residents had seen more of the world than the average cosmopolitan city-dweller. So while much of the whisky would have been drunk neat, there's a good chance that someone would have recognised this fashionable American cocktail as a fantastic celebration piece – and a good way to warm up after a night in the oil-slicked hold.

BLUE BLAZER: THE ORIGINAL

(Use two large silver-plated mugs)
Take 1 small tea-spoonful of powdered white sugar
dissolved in 1 wine-glass of boiling water.
1 wine-glass of Scotch whiskey.

Put the whisky and the boiling water in one mug, ignite the liquid with fire, and while blazing mix both ingredients by pouring them four or five times from one mug to the other. If well done this will have the appearance of a continued stream of liquid fire.

Serve in a small bar-glass with a piece of twisted lemon peel.

The novice in mixing this beverage should be careful not to scald himself. To become proficient in throwing the liquid from one mug to the other, it will be necessary to practise for some time with cold water.

Jerry Thomas, Bartender's Guide *(1887 reprint)*

THE ALCHEMIST'S VERSION

1 tsp caster sugar
50ml boiling water (or 40ml if your whisky is not cask strength)
50ml good single malt, ideally cask strength
Twist of lemon peel

Take two stainless-steel jugs with handles (the small ones used by baristas for steaming milk are ideal), and ensure that you are standing on a non-flammable surface and have someone on standby to put you out if this performance drink goes horribly wrong.

Add the sugar and boiling water to one jug, and stir until dissolved. Add the whisky, then light the mixture with a long

225

match. Very carefully pass it back and forth from one jug to the other in a small river of blue flame. Keep the pouring distance very small. Do not try to achieve the metre-long stream that Jerry Thomas could reputedly manage on your first attempt.

Put the mixture out by covering the full jug with the base of the empty one and pour into a heatproof glass, or perhaps a nice tankard that you've rescued from the officer's dining room. Add the twist of lemon peel and serve while still nicely warm.

Sip slowly, savouring the taste of the good rescued whisky and thinking about the adventures on an oil-slicked wreck that brought it to you.

For two days the islanders had the run of the *Politician*, as Charles McColl mistakenly believed that the weather was too bad for anyone to risk the run. But on the third day he hired a motorboat, the *St Joseph*, and made his first trip out on the hunt for looters, in the company of the Lochboisdale police constable Donald MacKenzie.

They soon came upon a heavily laden sailing ship, heading away from the *Politician*. The eight South Uist men on board didn't try to argue when McColl asked for their names and demanded that they hand over the twenty cases of whisky they carried, even though between them, they could easily have overpowered the two officers. (This pattern would repeat itself in all future captures: the islanders would do their best to hide the whisky, but would never fight when caught. They were firm in their belief that what they were doing was not wrong and should not be considered a crime, but at the same time they would never harm an officer of the law, or try to evade a court summons.)

Having taken the names and cargo, McColl had to leave quickly, trusting the men to return to shore, since he had already spotted another boat headed away from the *Politician*. It was travelling at top speed – the crew had already spotted him – but a sailing boat was no match for a motorboat, and the revenue officer soon caught up to them and boarded. The crew had briefly considered throwing the cases overboard for later retrieval but had decided against it, so they too lost their cargo and had their names taken to bring charges later. Finally the *St Joseph* landed on South Uist, and McColl walked alone to the nearest inn to phone in the charges and get the Home Guard to bring a truck to transport the seized whisky. On his way, he encountered a third boat which had already begun unloading, and he added another seven cases to his evening's seizures.

All eighteen of the men who were caught that evening were brought to court on charges of common theft – much to the dismay of Charles McColl, who had wanted them brought up on the more serious charge of defrauding the Revenue. Of the eight men from the first boat, two were given small fines and the other six were sentenced to thirty days in Inverness jail. From the crew of the second boat only one man was jailed, while the others all got away with the uniquely Scottish verdict of 'not proven'. Sadly, the only records that survive are of the verdicts, so we will probably never know how the other four got one man to take the rap for all of them. The third boat was an easy decision for a sympathetic magistrate. Since McColl had left his constable behind, he was the only witness to the seizure, and one witness didn't meet the legal requirement for collaboration – therefore all five were found 'not proven'.

Although three boats were only a small proportion of the huge number making visits to the *Politician*, this was to be Charles McColl's best day of hunting. He was unable to persuade Archie McIsaac, owner of the *St Joseph*, to hire out the boat again; Archie always told him that the weather was too bad, even though the crews rescuing the whisky clearly thought it was still worth the risk. He may have been afraid for the safety of his boat in high-speed chases, or he may have been persuaded not to help in the capture of his friends and neighbours, but either way, McColl was confined to land. He set about systematically searching the crofts of South Uist, where he lived, for contraband, accompanied by his trusty constable. They found a huge variety of items from the ship: bed springs, soap, chains, ink, disinfectant, mattresses, shovels, cloth, lamp wick, erasers, notebooks, even some signalling rockets – but only three bottles of whisky.

Later, McColl took to standing on the shore on high ground, looking out for boats that were leaving the *Politician* and then chasing them down to their landing places. A two-and-a-half-mile walk over bog and moor netted him two small boys, brothers, with a sack of sherry; but their adult supervisor managed to escape. The boys were charged, and it was the duty of John MacInnes, local government officer and general man-of-all-trades when it came to legal and bureaucratic duties on the island, to call on their mother and let her know about the charges. He arrived in the company of his good friend the local minister, who also had business with the boys' mother and had suggested they travel together.

Unfortunately, seeing the local government official and the minister approaching together did not go down well with the woman, who also had two other sons away serving in the army. She assumed the worst and went into hysterics, throwing herself around the croft and weeping, before the real news could be delivered. By the time the men had managed to calm her and let her know the reason they were visiting, neither had any will left to scold the boys as they had first intended, and they swiftly left the family in peace.

Meanwhile, McColl's demands for backup to help stop the constant flow of whisky out of the *Politician* had finally met with some success. He received, for one day, the help of an inspector from Lochmaddy, a sergeant from Barra and two customs men from Stornoway, along with Ian Gledhill, his immediate superior and the Portree Supervisor, who had already been lending an occasional hand when his other duties allowed. Together, the group took a boat across to Eriskay to make a thorough search of the crofts there. As soon as their approach was spotted, there were people running in every direction; it was the first customs presence that had been seen on Eriskay since the crash, and the residents hadn't been as careful as their neighbours on South Uist, who knew they had an officer living among them. A significant quantity of cases was seized, and a number of charges were brought. Once the whisky had all been shipped back to Lochboisdale it filled the cells, the office and even the policeman's garage and house.

The citizens of Eriskay spent the next few days in a state of paranoia, desperate to conceal any cases that hadn't yet been taken. One of the most popular hiding places was behind the wood panelling that lined most of the stone crofts; another was in the gaps beneath the floorboards. One cache of bottles was so well hidden beneath the floorboards of an Eriskay house that it was only discovered when some renovation work was done in 1990, and a neat little cubby was revealed containing two full and two half bottles of White Horse. Bottles retrieved in the past by divers had sold at over £4,000 at auction, and they had been in much worse condition; but the owner of this house was determined not to sell, and gave them to a local museum instead.

More temporary locations used to stash bottles included peat stacks, haystacks and even the rabbit holes out on the machair. The latter were such popular hiding places that when one resident took his case of King's Ransom out to hide it, he found that every hole was already full. He was forced to abandon the case, though not before having a long farewell drink that left him almost crawling back home.

Many people also sent bottles to friends and relatives on the mainland, simply by putting them in the post – until McColl got wind of the scheme, and demanded that the local postmaster start checking parcels and handing any suspicious packages in to him. The postmaster refused to make any seizures, but he did start advising anyone who arrived with a whisky-shaped parcel that they might be better off taking it home again, as it was likely to be checked at the sorting office.

There was just one act of retaliation against Charles McColl: late one night, someone climbed onto the roof of his garage and drilled a hole, then poured paraffin through it all over the car inside and set it alight. The blaze was swiftly spotted by some local fishermen and extinguished, but if it had not been so quickly dealt with, it could easily have spread to the house. As it was, only one of the two cars in the garage was damaged (and even that was the wrong car; the other one was McColl's).

Most people who had 'rescued' the whisky kept it for their own personal use, or gave it away to friends; but there were, inevitably, a handful of others who attempted to make money from it. The Ministry of Defence was in the process of building an airstrip up at Benbecula, the next island north of South Uist and one without a single public house to its name. Once they heard about the wreck of the *Politician*, the thirsty and well-paid navvies doing the building work began to drive across the causeway down to

South Uist every weekend, waving their money about and buying up cases of whisky from anyone who would sell to them. Soon a few enterprising locals began taking trucks of whisky up to Benbecula to sell direct – a traffic that Charles McColl tried to stop, but without much success.

The closest he came was on one occasion when the driver of a whisky-running truck spotted a police car, and got nervous. If his nerves hadn't caused him to speed up, the police probably wouldn't have taken any notice of him, but his suspicious behaviour attracted their attention and soon they were chasing him down the island's narrow lanes. The driver was close to the airport and had a good lead, but the roads were flat and straight, so he had no chance of getting out of sight of the police and losing them. Instead he made straight for the building works, in the hope of getting the navvies to help him quickly hide the whisky. However, when he arrived there was no one in sight except the driver of a single bulldozer, spreading tarmac across the newly laid foundations of the runway. Backing the truck up to the runway, the driver emptied his cargo onto the foundations, where the bulldozer promptly covered it over. When the police arrived shortly afterwards, no evidence remained for them to find.

If you ever visit Benbecula, spare a moment to think of the thirty cases of good whisky that are forever trapped beneath your wheels as you land. That poor buried whisky would never see even the simplest of cocktails – not even this one, which had already earned the moniker 'Old Fashioned' by the 1880s, and yet still graces every good cocktail menu more than 130 years later. It's a shame, since it would have been the perfect drink to show off the excellent qualities of that high-class millionaire's market whisky, rescued from the ocean only to be trapped in tarmac.

OLD FASHIONED COCKTAIL: THE ORIGINAL

1 lump of sugar

2 dashes Angostura Bitters

2 oz Rye Whisky

Crush sugar and bitters together, add a lump of ice, decorate with a twist of lemon peel and a slice of orange using a medium-size glass, and stir well. This cocktail can be made with Brandy, Gin, Rum, etc. instead of Rye Whisky.

Harry Craddock, from The Savoy Cocktail Book *(1930)*

THE ALCHEMIST'S VERSION

25ml sugar syrup

50ml good single malt whisky

3–4 drops bitters of your choice

4–5 cubes ice

Make the sugar syrup by dissolving 100g sugar in 100ml boiling water, and allowing to cool. The rest of the syrup can be saved in the

*fridge for another day. Then simply add all the ingredients to a short
tumbler and stir well for 20–30 seconds, until properly chilled.*

On 12 May, just over three months after the wreck of the
Politician, the shipbreakers arrived to salvage what they could
of the iron and steel of the ship. To the surprise of many,
they declared that, with enough patching and pumping in
of air, they could actually refloat the entire ship and tow
it away to the mainland, where it could be fully broken up
for scrap. Charles McColl was overjoyed: it seemed that
the troublesome whisky might at last be towed out of his
jurisdiction forever. He even extracted a promise from the
workers that while they were removing the remaining cargo
to lighten the ship for refloating, they would pay special
attention to the contents of hold number five and send the
whisky back to Glasgow under a customs seal.

The first few loads were transferred onto boats and
dumped straight into the holds in whatever condition they
came out of the *Politician*, unsorted and covered with oil.
They were sealed and taken back to Glasgow, although the
salvors and the boat crews continued helping themselves
with no regard for the seals. The few cases that were deemed
rescuable were loaded onto trains to be returned to the
same warehouses they had come from – only for the seals
to be broken again, and the whisky liberally pilfered, by
the railway men. By the time the remainder limped its way

into the warehouses and the stewardship of the Revenue, they had given up all hope of charging excise duty on the total original cargo of the ship, which would have been standard practice; they simply wanted to write off the whole episode as soon as possible. The salvors were instructed to throw any more cases they recovered into the sea rather than bother bringing them back – although that would only serve to further justify the islanders' claims that they were 'rescuing' the whisky rather than stealing it.

By the time the salvors were ready to attempt the refloating, it was estimated that there were still around 4,000 cases left on board, not to mention thousands of loose bottles from broken cases lying in the bottom of the hold. Still, on 22 September, after four months of work removing cargo, welding the torn hull and pumping the holds full of compressed air, the *Politician* finally floated free of the rocks that had caught her more than six months earlier. She might have left the islands forever that day, if the salvage crew had not disagreed about whether it was safe to tow her all the way to the mainland immediately. Caution won out, and she was let down again on a sandbank, where it was thought she could safely rest until the weather was better for the journey. Unfortunately there was a large rock lurking unseen in the middle of the sandbank, which broke the back of the ship and made refloating impossible – a sad end to four months of work. The only way to salvage some value from the failed operation was to cut the ship in half and refloat the more intact front section only, leaving the more badly damaged rear section – including hold number five – behind on the ocean floor.

Charles McColl turned then to his final option: complete destruction of the ship's cargo. He requested, and, after several months of waiting, received, permission to put the whisky beyond use by dynamiting the hold. On 6 August 1942, divers took sixteen sticks of gelignite down into the hold and put the remainder of the cargo to rest. The explosion was audible for miles, and no doubt many took a moment from their work to mourn the passing of those 4,000 remaining cases of whisky.

In the wartime news blackout, the story of the ship-wrecked whisky might have remained nothing more than a local legend – had there not been a famous comic novelist, Compton Mackenzie, living in seclusion on Eriskay. He chose to write a fictionalised version of the story – the crash of the SS *Cabinet Minister* – which became a novel so successful that it made his previous fame look tame in comparison. *Whisky Galore* was published in 1947, and has since sold over 200,000 copies and been translated into many different languages. In 1949, even more lasting fame was assured when the film adaptation became the first Ealing Comedy to be filmed on location, causing much local bemusement as the film company winched fibreglass rocks over the existing local ones, which were 'not rugged enough'.

Since then, several writers have made in-depth attempts to get to the bottom of the story of the real Whisky Galore. I am indebted to them for recording the first-hand accounts of those who have since passed beyond the ability to tell their stories, and away into enduring Scottish legend. The most seminal of these works is Arthur Swinson's 1963 book, named after a supposed exchange between the director of *Whisky Galore* and the American humorist James Thurber, who was unimpressed by the title given to the US release of the film: *Tight Little Island*. 'I wish I'd known you at the time,' Thurber supposedly said. 'The right American title for the film is *Scotch on the Rocks*' – and so that, instead, ended up as the title of Swinson's book. It is filled with anecdotes that he charmed from the Eriskay inhabitants, even though there was still a chance they could be prosecuted for the crimes he was writing about. This cocktail is my tribute to him.

SCOTCH ON THE ROCKS: THE ALCHEMIST'S VERSION

2–3 drops salt solution
3–4 cubes good clear ice
50ml whisky

First make up the salt solution by dissolving a tablespoon of salt in 50ml of hot water and allowing it to cool. Drop the ice into a tumbler and pour the whisky over it. Add 2–3 drops of the salt solution with a pipette if you have one, or by carefully dripping from a teaspoon if not.

Stir well and enjoy, accompanied by a good Scottish fairy tale.

CHAPTER EIGHT

EXPLODING GARAGES
AND BOOTLEG BRANDS

y the start of the twentieth century, food safety laws, which were first introduced in 1860, had made legal spirits reliably safe. Illicit spirits were suddenly shockingly dangerous by comparison, and it took the restrictions and deprivations of two world wars to persuade the public to return to drinking them. When those restrictions were lifted, this late burst of enthusiasm, or arguably of desperation, for illicit spirits faded away.

Now, with legal spirits freely available in all their forms, public concern about the safety of our food and drink, and the growth of the organic food movement, there is an outcry verging on panic at the slightest hint of tainted food. So what place can there possibly be for illicit spirits? Surely they are only still with us as a piece of theatre – as a way of playing at being naughty to make a trip to an otherwise legal bar more thrilling, or connecting with our outlaw ancestors.

A strong, united culture of illegal distilling certainly no longer exists in Britain today as it did in Scotland or Ireland in the 1700s. But that doesn't mean that there aren't any individuals producing illicit spirits. There are plenty of people working away in sheds and kitchens, producing very small amounts of drink for themselves and their friends, just for the sheer enjoyment of making it. Most aren't even aware that they are doing anything illegal, or at least would likely claim not to be. It's simply another hobby to them, such as home brewing, gardening or knitting. They certainly aren't selling their wares commercially.

The internet has allowed this kind of illicit distilling to become more accessible than ever before – but that hasn't made it any less illegal. HMRC will occasionally crack down on the websites selling compact 'water purifiers', which just happen to work by distillation, or pot stills that are 'for decorative purposes only' but by coincidence are also fully operational. However, government intervention is little more than a token effort and the trade is not really regarded as a priority. There are much worse things for sale on the internet than stills, and in any case, trying to shut anything down online is a little bit like trying to plug all the holes in a sieve. On the whole, unless the hobbyists actually poison themselves, blow themselves up, start selling their produce or otherwise make themselves too public to ignore, the authorities tend to leave them to their own devices.

It may sound like we should all go out and get a micro still, but the ones used by hobbyists tend to produce either a very rough spirit or one that has been completely stripped of flavour and character by filtering. Essences are available to give the spirit the flavour of rum, gin, whisky or various liqueurs (they use the same artificial flavourings as baking and are perfectly safe, especially compared to the turpentine used in earlier times) but they are a long way from the real thing in taste, besides guaranteeing that your 'unique' homemade spirit tastes exactly the same as everyone else's. Between the poor quality of the product, the high cost of the equipment and the amount of time it takes to produce only a small quantity of spirit, the garden-shed distillers really do have to be doing it for fun rather than trying to make a cheap drink. It would take a very heavy drinker to make back the cost of the equipment – and even then they might struggle to produce as fast as they could drink.

The cost factor is the main reason why the culture of illicit distilling died out. In the past, for many people, legal spirits would have been both prohibitively expensive and difficult to obtain, particularly when certain kinds of spirit were banned. But now, legal spirits are affordable and easily available to the vast majority of the population.

Although spirits are cheap to the consumer compared to incomes, duty remains high: as much as 75 per cent of the cost of the cheapest bottle of vodka might be duty. To avoid that cost, there are unscrupulous traders who are willing to put illegal products into the market to improve their margins and make a quick profit, letting their customers shoulder the risk of potentially dangerous spirits, which they might not have bought if they had known the origin.

Some of it might even be safe, although it certainly isn't legal. Thousands of bottles of legitimately produced spirit leave the UK every year with no duty paid on them, going off for sale in other countries that would then charge their own duty. The easiest method of avoiding the tax is to turn a few of those deliveries around and apply fake duty stamps, swiftly turning legal exports into illegal 'diverted' spirits – but it is also the riskiest. The crime leaves a paper trail of export licences and shipment numbers, and it needs to take place in and around registered bonded warehouses, which are liable to regular spot checks. It is also only worth doing in high volume: with profits of around £5 a bottle on spirits, the profit-to-volume ratios are very low compared with the smuggling of drugs or even of duty-unpaid cigarettes. But large quantities are hard to hide – especially when crossing national borders, which greatly increases the chance of getting caught.

Even creative solutions don't pay off. Two brothers from Rochdale were jailed in 2013 after they constructed a second, secret warehouse behind the bonded warehouse of their legitimate wholesale business. They were part of a huge, organised duty-evasion ring: spirits produced in Scotland were brought into the registered warehouse on their way to be exported to Belgium, but while in the warehouse part of the consignment was diverted. Inside a shower cubicle there was a secret entrance: in true Scooby-Doo style intrigue, swivelling a particular hook opened up the side wall to reveal the hidden doorway. Cases were carried through to the second warehouse, where the spirits were relabelled as UK duty paid. When the premises were raided in 2009, there were over 12,000 bottles concealed inside.

The hiding place in the warehouse might have been well concealed but masking the wider network of the operation was more challenging and where the pair ultimately failed. One of their employees had been under surveillance for months by a joint HMRC and UK Border Force team under the name Operation Installbox. They had discovered that he had links to another larger gang, which had been broken up by an earlier operation.

More dangerous than smuggling is the illegal production of spirits. The risks are much greater than loss of money or liberty as much of the product poses a serious danger to consumers – but also to the producers. On 13 July 2011, a garage in the Broadfield Lane industrial estate in Boston, Lincolnshire, exploded. One man escaped from the fireball with his arms ablaze while five others were killed instantly. The explosion was audible five miles away and the fire burned so intensely that the metal doors of the unit warped and buckled, a car outside spontaneously caught alight in the heat and most of the evidence inside was destroyed. At the inquest held into the deaths, the lone survivor gave evidence that the men had been running an illegal still inside the unit and smoking while they worked.

Although those deaths were a tragedy, at least the incident meant that the vodka they were producing was kept out of the market. Six days after the explosion, an industrial unit in Brewery Street, Birmingham, was raided and a gang was discovered producing bootleg vodka under the invented brand name Arctic Ice. Running a still makes it more likely that an operation will be caught, so the gang were instead faking the vodka by diluting down industrial alcohol, containing high levels of deadly methanol. By the time the plant was discovered, the vodka was already in circulation, although it was easily identifiable by the invented brand name, and officers went out searching for the product further down the retail chain. Their search also found substantial quantities of counterfeit Glen's Vodka, which contained not only high levels of methanol but also traces of chloroform.

As one of the cheapest brand names on the high street, Glen's has often found itself the brand of choice for bootleggers, to the great frustration and annoyance of the genuine producer. A bottling plant in Derbyshire was making counterfeit Glen's when it was raided in December 2014. The vodka had been produced by running antifreeze through reverse osmosis units to remove the colour and smell but the process was clearly not working well enough as a customer reported a suspect bottle of vodka to his local Trading Standards office, telling them that it smelt like nail varnish remover. No full bottles were found on the premises, only more than 20,000 empties waiting to be filled and hundreds of empty five-litre antifreeze bottles which had already been used to make the counterfeit Glen's. That meant there were bottles already sitting in off-licences, bars and clubs, waiting for an unsuspecting public.

There are often clear signs for proprietors that a spirit is not legitimate, but some choose to ignore them. The Ttonic Bar in Sunderland was caught in a regular spot check by HMRC in June 2014 when an unusually large quantity (450 litres) of duty-unpaid spirit was found on the premises. Some was safe European stock but there was also dangerous bootleg vodka, confirmed as fake by an expert witness from the Loch Lomond Group, which owns Glen's Vodka. Part of the consignment had already been served to customers. The landlady pleaded in court that the drink had been bought in good faith, but the court ruled for the prosecution, who claimed that the low price should have made the origin clear, as well as the suspicious actions of the supplier who refused to give his full name, would only take cash and gave no receipts or invoices.

That raid was far from a one-off incident. Another sweep in South Lanarkshire and Glasgow in September 2013 seized 1,282 litres of spirits, and that was just one of over 100 similar taskforce sweeps launched between 2011 and 2015. Total seizures in just one year amounted to over 12 million litres of alcohol (although that figure does include illegal wine and beer as well as spirits), and it is estimated that in 2010 as many as one in four off-licences were selling counterfeit or diverted alcohol. The largest operation was discovered in 2007 in Dalston Lane, Hackney, where a two-storey factory was using industrial alcohol smuggled from Eastern Europe and fake packaging produced in Cyprus to churn out twenty-four bottles every minute, all branded as Smirnoff, Kirov and Glen's. The factory, described by the arresting officers as 'rat-infested', had been running for two years before it was discovered.

While the UK-based managers of these operations were caught, their financiers were not, and the international nature of their supply lines suggested serious backers were involved. These factories were not ramshackle affairs where bottles were filled by amateurs with funnels, but full-scale production lines using industrial bottling and labelling machines, implying serious investment. The frequency, size and similarity of the bootlegging operations that are discovered, raided and then swiftly re-established else-where, suggest that they are run by serious organised crime networks. Unlike the smugglers and illicit distillers of the past, these networks are apart from the community rather than a part of it, with the public positioned as their victims rather than their co-conspirators or even their willing cus-tomers. Consumers are often unaware that they are buying potentially deadly products, without any knowledge of their origin or the danger that they pose, with effects ranging from a bad hangover to coma or permanent blindness.

To keep yourself safe when buying spirits, the Food Standards Agency advises people to look closely at labels to check that they are straight and properly attached, and to keep an eye out for spelling mistakes. The counterfeit Glen's from the Derbyshire haul, for example, was easily identified by the word 'bottled' on the label, which was misspelt as 'botteled'. Glen's have also recently introduced embossing on their bottles to make counterfeiting more difficult. You can also check that all the bottles of the same brand in the shop look the same and are filled to the same level. The colour and smell are often not quite right – keep a lookout for a brownish or yellowish tinge, cloudiness or a smell similar to nail varnish remover. If you find a bottle you think is suspicious you can call the FSA for further assistance. Ultimately, the general advice from Trading Standards is that if an offer looks too good to be true, it probably is.

But it's not just the cheap bottle of vodka in your corner shop which may turn out to be a fake. There is also a growing problem at the high end of the whisky market with counterfeit old and rare bottles being sold at auction for large sums of money. In 2016 the whisky brokerage firm Rare Whisky 101 published a shocking exposé after purchasing over £1 millon of whisky at auction which they tested and proved to be fake. The fakes included what was supposedly a 1903 bottle of Laphroaig. It would have been the oldest bottle in existence had it proved to be genuine and was valued at over £100,000 for the single bottle but sadly proved not even to be a single malt, let alone over 100 years old. The tests they used to prove the whiskies were fakes ranged from simple expert examination of the labelling for flaws and inconsistencies, to radiocarbon dating performed by a team Oxford University. Between the cost of the testing and the cost of purchasing the suspected fakes at auction the whole exercise was a very expensive way of marketing the testing and authentication services which they offer.

The same firm were called in to perform the testing when the authenticity of the most expensive single dram that had ever been sold, costing a mind-blowing 10,000 Swiss francs (or around £7,600), was called into question by experts who read reports of the sale in the media in 2017. The dram was purchased by Zhang Wei, a writer of martial arts fantasy novels and one of the highest-earning online writers in China. The writer was drinking at the Devil's Place bar in St Moritz, which has a collection of over 2,500 different whiskies. The collection included a bottle of 1878 Macallan single malt which was purchased by the manager's father, who had also managed the bar, in the 1990s and had never been opened.

The bottle was on display but was not listed on the menu and the manager, Sandro Bernasconi, had never even thought to open it but when Zhang Wei asked to try it, and agreed to the high price asked, the manager called his father who encouraged him to open the bottle. His father told him, 'We could wait another twenty years for a customer like that, so we should sell it.' The story has a partially happy ending since Mr Bernasconi sent the whisky for testing as soon as the authenticity was questioned. When it was revealed to be a fake he flew straight out to China to personally offer a refund to the writer who then thanked him for his scrupulous honesty.

While the idea of a rich collector shelling out thousands for what may turn out to be a dressed-up bottle of Bells, and being unable to tell the difference, is ultimately harmless and even hilarious there is no romance or plucky under-dog involved in the industrial production lines which are churning out cheap spirits that the producers know to be dangerous. And yet although we reject the modern reality of illicit spirit production, for some reason we still crave a taste of that imagined past where all smugglers were rosy-cheeked, honest scoundrels who were pluckily facing off against the moustache-twirling, oppressive evil of the establishment. And there's no harm in wanting to do that, just as we want to play at medieval sword fighting without the mud and blood, or recreate Elizabethan banquets without the subsequent tooth decay. We can take inspiration from the past without needing to faithfully recreate all of its faults.

Luckily a class of bar has sprung up to offer us the thrill of that history without the risk or the hard edges, one which also often serves cocktails so good that they win international awards. The modern speakeasy bar is the per-fect rollercoaster of wrongdoing: all of the excitement of breaking the law but with the safety bars firmly locked in place to keep you safe from harm.

The speakeasy trend began almost by accident, but the speed with which it spread internationally revealed that there was a desire waiting to be met. On New Year's Eve in 1999, a bar called Milk & Honey opened in New York. The owner of the building hadn't been keen on having a bar in the small basement room but the bartender was a friend and in the end he agreed, provided the bar was quiet and was kept well out of sight so that it would not upset the residents.

As a result, the original Milk & Honey only had twenty tables and a door that was completely unmarked. You had to have a reservation to drink and bookings could only be made by phone, on a number that changed on a regular basis and was never advertised, only passed on by word of mouth. The bar also had no menu (a quirk that the owner claims came about because he couldn't work a laser printer), but the bartender would make any classic drink on request or recommend one based on your preferences. Well-made classics available outside of hotel bars (and hotel bar prices) were rare, and it was that combined with the thrill of the discovery of the venue that turned Milk & Honey into the global phenomenon it became, which would inspire a worldwide trend.

With the classic cocktail revival in full swing, there was also a renewed interest in the spirits that go into a classic. Microdistilleries had already sprung up in America on the back of the microbrewery movement, mostly producing traditional American spirits like rye, but gin had been out of fashion for so long, only the big international brands were producing it. Now there was a market for a local craft gin to rival those brands. By 2005 there were several American small batch gins but there was still nothing coming out of Britain, the original home of the spirit.

The trend for small batch gin was slow in making it home across the Atlantic because, as far as HMRC was concerned, the regulations brought in to put a halt to the gin craze more than 200 years previously were still in force. HMRC insisted that the minimum allowed size for a still was 18 hectolitres, or 1,800 litres, which was far too much to be considered a small batch.

But the spirit of rebellion had not been completely quelled, and, finally, in 2007 someone came along with the funds and the willingness to fight HMRC until they won. When Sipsmith tried to set up the first small pot still to produce gin in London in 200 years and were told that the ban on distilling gin in small quantities was still in place they began a two-year legal battle to get that ban overturned. When they finally opened their doors in 2009 they set a legal precedent that would allow for a craft spirit boom which has still not reached its peak.

In addition to Sipsmith there are now more than a dozen working distilleries in London alone, all of which are unique and many of which are open to the public. I will highlight those that are not necessarily the best but are the ones I know best. The rest you will have to seek out for yourselves, and it will be a quest worth pursuing.

Jensen's was founded in 2004, produced by a contract distiller before the microdistillery ban was broken, with a London Dry that aimed to recreate the style of 'vintage' gins produced in the 1960s and 70s. They have since gone further back in time, lovingly recreating an Old Tom recipe from an eighteenth-century distillers' notebook. Ten years later they opened their own distillery which is now open to the public at the weekends, providing the drinks to go with the good food at the neighbouring Maltby Street Market.

Sacred, on the contrary, is never open to the public as their range of beautiful oddities have been produced by Ian Hart from a vacuum still on his kitchen table since 2009, making him one of the earliest to set up after the ban was overturned. The vacuum still allows the gin to be distilled at a much lower temperature, producing a different flavour profile to a normal pot still gin. While Sacred Gin has the words 'gin' and 'London dry' on the label, it is debatable whether the technique used (distilling each botanical individually and then blending the results) prevents Sacred from calling itself a 'London dry gin'. To make up for that Ian has trademarked the term 'London dry vodka'.

One of my favourite newcomers is 58 Gin, because alongside their commercial still they have installed six miniature stills, capable of producing only two bottles in each distillation. If you book tickets to their distillery experience then you get to operate those stills yourself and produce a bottle of your very own gin to take home. It's safer, easier and much more legal than trying to make your own at home.

The last London distillery I must mention is East London Liquor Company. I am far too prejudiced to be believed when I tell you how great this distillery is, as I'm very closely connected to them, but I can say with certainty that they are currently producing the first whisky distilled in East London in over a hundred years. For the rest you will just have to stop by the bar, which is open seven days a week, and taste the range of spirits for yourself while watching the three copper stills gleam through the glass wall at the back. Then you can make up your own mind.

However, the new distilleries aren't just confined to London. There's Brighton Gin in Brighton; Bramley and Gage in Bristol; The Cambridge Distillery in Cambridge; Curio, Elemental, The Wrecking Coast and Southwestern Distillery in Cornwall; Salcombe Gin in Devon; Conker in Dorset; The Durham Distillery in Durham; Wicked Wolf on Exmoor; Whittaker's in Harrogate; Puddingstone Distillery in Hertfordshire; The Isle of Wight distillery on The Isle of Wight; Forest Gin in Macclesfield; Dancing Cows in The New Forest; Warner Edwards in Northamptonshire; Hepple Gin in Northumbria; North Star and The Dyfi Distillery in North Wales; The Shakespeare Distillery in Stratford-upon-Avon; Poetic License in Sunderland; Silent Pool in Surrey and Masons in Yorkshire, to list just a fraction of this new wave of dreamers and experimenters in England and Wales in all their great variety.

Finally there is Scotland, which was already the world's largest producer of London Dry Gin as most of the larger brands have actually been produced in Scotland for many years. Not content to fall behind in the new craft gin race there have been both new distilleries founded dedicated to gin, such as Pickering's in Edinburgh, and new craft gins produced by old whisky distilleries, such as The Botanist coming out of the Bruichladdich distillery on Islay. But prize for the best pun goes to El:gin produced in the town of Elgin, Speyside. Scotland has also seen a flourishing of new, small whisky distilleries. With the age requirements for whisky it will be a while longer before they all make it to the shelves but we should brace ourselves because the forty new distilleries opened in 2015 should all be reaching the legal minimum age sometime this year.

In total, taking gin and whisky together, 157 distilleries opened in the UK between 2010 and 2016, more than doubling the total number. With such a booming industry we are now living in a real golden age with every taste catered for and no need to take the risks involved in making our own. And if you still can't resist the urge to experiment after trying the wide range available then there are even several legal options for making your own gin, with the guidance of an experienced distiller to make sure you end up with a good product.

If we largely have no need for illicit spirits now, that's not because the craft and passion that once went into them have gone away – rather, they've gone legitimate. But, should anyone ever dare to try take our spirits away again, they will always be waiting for us.

RECOMMENDED FURTHER READING

If you would like to learn more about the historical eras covered in this book the author recommends the following:

Dillon, Patrick, *The Much Lamented Death of Madam Geneva: The Eighteenth-century Gin Craze* (London: Headline Review, 2002)

Hewett, E. H. and Axton, W. F., *Convivial Dickens: The Drinks of Dickens & His Times* (Athens, Ohio: Ohio University Press, 1985)

Hutchinson, Roger, *Polly: The True Story Behind Whisky Galore* (Edinburgh: Mainstream Publishing, 1990)

Mackenzie, Compton, *Whisky Galore* (Edinburgh: Birlinn, 2012)

McGuffin, John, *In Praise of Poteen* (Belfast: Appletree Press, 1978)

Minnick, Fred, *Whisky Women: The Untold Story of How Women Saved Bourbon, Scotch and Irish Whisky* (Lincoln, Nebraska: Potomac Books Inc, 2013)

Platt, Richard, *Smuggling in the British Isles: A History* (Stroud: The History Press, 2011)

Rowett Johns, Jeremy, *The Smugglers' Banker: The Story of Zephaniah Job of Polperro* (Clifton-upon-Teme: Polperro Heritage Press, 1997)

Smith, Gavin D., *The Scottish Smuggler* (Edinburgh: Birlinn, 2003)

Smith, Gavin D., *The Secret Still: Scotland's Clandestine Whisky Makers* (Edinburgh: Birlinn, 2002)

Swinson, Arthur, *Scotch on the Rocks: The True Story Behind Whisky Galore* (London: Peter Davies, 1963)

Thomas, Donald, *An Underworld at War: Spivs, Deserters, Racketeers and Civilians in the Second World War* (London: John Murray, 2004)

Townsend, Brian, *Scotch Missed: Scotland's Lost Distilleries* (Castle Douglas: The Angel's Share, 2000)

Trow, M. J., *War Crimes: Underworld Britain in the Second World War* (Barnsley: Pen & Sword Aviation, 2008)

Waugh, Mary, *Smuggling in Devon & Cornwall 1700–1850* (Newbury: Countryside Books, 1991)

Waugh, Mary, *Smuggling in Kent & Sussex 1700–1840* (Newbury: Countryside Books, 1985)

Warner, Jessica, *Craze: Gin and Debauchery in an Age of Reason* (London: Profile Books, 2003)

Wilson, Anne, *Water of Life: A History of Wine-Distilling and Spirits* (London: Prospect Books, 2006)

Wondrich, David, *Imbibe!* (London: Perigee, 2007)

Wondrich, David, *Punch: The Delights and Dangers of the Flowing Bowl* (London: Perigee, 2010)

Sources for material used

Barnard, Alfred, *The Whisky Distilleries of the United Kingdom* (London: Harper's Weekly Gazette, 1887)

Boyle, P., *The Publican and Spirit Dealer's Daily Companion, or, plain and interesting advice to wine vault and public house keepers, On subjects of the greatest Importance to their own Welfare, and to the Health, Comfort & Satisfaction Of Their Customers & Society At Large* (Sixth Edition, c. 1800)

Butler, Isaac, *Journey Through Fermanagh* (1760)

Campbell, Walter, *The Old Forest Ranger* (London: Routledge, 1850)

Cook, R. *Oxford Night Caps: A Collection of Receipts for Making Various Beverages* (Oxford: Henry Slatter, 1827)

Glasse, Hannah, *The Art of Cookery Made Plain and Easy* (1747)

Heath, Ambrose, *Two Hundred War-Time Recipes – From the Kitchen Front* (London: Eyre & Spottiswoode, 1941)

Lewis, Dr John, *A Doctor's Occupation* (London: New English Library, 1982)

MacDonald, Aeneas, *Whisky* (Edinburgh: Porpoise Press, 1930)

Osgood Mackenzie, *A Hundred Years in the Highlands* (London: Edwin Arnold, 1921)

Plat, Hugh, *Sundrie New and Artificiall Remedies against Famine* (London: 1596)

Thomas, Jerry, *Bartender's Guide* (New York: Dick & Fitzgerald, 1887 reprint)

Apicius (c. 4th century)

Curye on Inglysch (c. 14th century)

Letter from Charles Dickens to Mrs F. (18 January 1847)

Logistics corps field manual (c. 1943)

Ministry of Food advisory (1943)

Notebook of William Worcester, (c. 1860–70)

The Savoy Cocktail Book (London: Constable & Co., 1930)

Lyrics to Spivs' Anthem on page 209 based on the song 'Side By Side' by Harry M. Woods © 1927 Shapiro Bernstein & Co. Inc New York

ACKNOWLEDGEMENTS

'd like to thank my agent Lydia Moed for picking up a ball which had been dropped for so long that I had almost forgotten about it altogether; without her, this book would never have been published. I also thank my editors Pippa and Jennie for making this a much better book than it could possibly have been had I been left without their help and guidance. They have been very kind to a chemistry graduate and bartender trying to produce my first piece of extended writing since school (my thesis doesn't count, it was mostly graphs and diagrams).

I also have to give huge thanks to my parents for their seemingly endless patience with my eccentric career choices. I know they are going to be proud to see my name in print.

Finally, my thanks go to my adventurous recipe testers: Dan Bailey, Erin Johnson, Will Blackstock, Gabrielle Osrin, Graham Charlton, Julia Savage, Ness Thompsett, Ruth Verlarde and Sarah Ferguson, who helped prevent disaster on a number of occasions. I hope their taste buds have suffered no permanent damage.

INDEX

INDEX

ABOUT THE AUTHOR

Ruth Ball works at East London Liquor Company, a London distillery. She is a chemist and former bartender, and was the founder of Alchemist Dreams, a company dedicated to making handmade liqueurs blended to order for high-profile creative events with The British Library, Starwood Hotels and The Science Museum Group. She is also the author of *Rough Spirits and High Society: The Culture of Drink*.